Swedish
Phrase Book
&
Dictionary

Berlitz Publishing
New York Munich Singapore

Contacting the Editors

Every effort has been made to provide accurate information in this publication, but changes are inevitable. The publisher cannot be responsible for any resulting loss, inconvenience or injury. We would appreciate it if readers would call our attention to any errors or outdated information. We also welcome your suggestions; if you come across a relevant expression not in our phrase book, please contact us: Berlitz Publishing, 193 Morris Avenue, Springfield, NJ 07081, USA. Email: comments@berlitzbooks.com.

Third Printing: May 2009
Printed in Singapore

Publishing Director: Sheryl Olinsky Borg
Project Manager: Farida Aslanova
Translation: Katarina E. Tucker
Composition: Datagrafix, Inc.
Cover Design: Claudia Petrilli
Interior Design: Derrick Lim, Juergen Bartz
Production Manager: Elizabeth Gaynor
Cover Photo: © picturesofeurope.co.uk/Alamy
Interior Photos: p. 14 © Studio Fourteen/Brand X Pictures/age fotostock; p. 19 © Sveriges Riksbank; p. 26 © Pixtal/age fotostock; p. 36 © Roman Korchuk, 2006/Shutterstock, Inc.; p. 39 © Corbis/fotosearch.com; p. 51 © Purestock/Alamy; p. 57 © Quendi Language Services; p. 60 © Stockbyte Photography/2002-07 Veer Incorporated; p.81 © Quendi Language Services; p. 92 © Javier Larrea/Pixtal/age fotostock; p. 95 © Netfalls/2003-2007 Shutterstock, Inc.; p. 119 © Kropotov Andrey/2003-2007 Shutterstock, Inc.; p. 122 © Imageshop.com; p. 126 © image100/Corbis; p. 129 © photodisc/2007 Punchstock; p.132 © 2007 Jupiterimages Corporation; p.136 © 2007 Jupiterimages Corporation; p.144 © David Dea/2003-2007 Shutterstock, Inc.; p.151 © 2007 Jupiterimages Corporation; p. 159 © Jupiterimages/Brand X/Corbis; p. 161 © Stockbyte/Fotosearch.com; p. 163 © Corbis/2006 JupiterImages Corporation; p.166 © David McKee/2003-2007 Shutterstock, Inc.; p. 168, 172, 186 © 2007 Jupiterimages Corporation; inside back cover: © H.W.A.C.

Contents

Survival

Food

People

Fun

Special Needs

Resources

Dictionary

Pronunciation

This section is designed to familiarize you with the sounds of Swedish using our simplified phonetic transcription. You'll find the pronunciation of the Swedish letters and sounds explained below, together with their "imitated" equivalents. To use this system, found throughout the phrase book, simply read the pronunciation as if it were English, noting any special rules below.

The Swedish alphabet has 29 letters, the last three of which are the vowels **å**, **ä** and **ö**. Unlike English, the letter **y** is a vowel, meaning that Swedish has nine vowels. Swedish vowels are pure vowel sounds, as opposed to being a combination of two sounds (diphthongs) as they often are in English. Diphthongs occur only in dialects such as **Gotländska** (spoken on the island of Gotland), **Skånska** (spoken in the southern province of Skåne) and **Dalmål** (spoken in Dalarna, a province roughly in the middle of the country.)

Swedish has very consistent rules with respect to the sounding of individual letters, i.e. all the letters should be pronounced distinctly, even vowels and consonants at the ends of words. The Swedish language is often referred to as a "musical" language due to the fact that the intonation and rhythm moves up and down, giving the language a musical quality. Despite this stress, like pronunciation, is quite consistent. Most words with two or more syllables have primary stress on the first syllable of the word, and this can be followed by a secondary stress on the second syllable. There are also a number of words with two or more syllables which do not have stress on the first syllable, but often on the last. Stress has been noted in the phonetic transcription with underlining.

Consonants

Letter	Approximate Pronunciation	Symbol	Example	Pronunciation
c	like s in sit	s	**cykel**	sew·kerl*
g	1. before o, å, a and u, like g in get	g	**gata**	gah·ta
	2. before i, e, ö and ä, like y in yet	y	**get**	yet
	3. after r and l, like y in yet	y	**borg**	bohry
j	1. soft, like y in yet	y	**jag**	yahg
	2. after r and l, like y in yet	y	**familj**	fah·mihly
k	1. before o, å, a and u, like k in keep	k	**katt**	kat
	2. before i, e, ö and ä, like ch in chew		**köpa**	chur·pa
q	like k in keep	k	**Blomquist**	bloom·kvihst
r	strong, almost trilled, r		**röd**	rurd
s	like s in see	s	**sitta**	siht·a

w	like v in very	v	**wennergren**	vehn•eh•grehn
z	like s in suit	s	**zebra**	see•bra

Letters b, d, f, h, m, n, p, t, v and x are generally pronounced as in English.

*Bold indicates a lengthening of the sound, an extra emphasis on the vowel sound.

Consonant Clusters

Letter	Approximate Pronunciation	Symbol	Example	Pronunciation
ch	like sh in ship	sh	**check**	shehk
ck	like ck in tick	k	**flicka**	flih•ka
dj, gj, hj, lj	like y in yet	y	**djur**	yeur
sj, skj, stj, sch, ch	like sh in shop	sh	**sjal**	shahl
sk	1. before o, å, a and u, like sk in skip	sk	**skala**	skah•la
	2. before i, e, ö and ä, like sh in ship	sh	**skära**	shai•ra
tj	like sh followed by ch	shch	**tjock**	shchohk

Vowels

Letter	Approximate Pronunciation	Symbol	Example	Pronunciation
a	1. when long, like a in father	ah	**dag**	dahg
	2. when short, like a in cat	a	**katt**	kat
e	1. when long, like ee in beer	ee	**veta**	vee•ta
	2. when short, like e in fell	eh	**ett**	eht
i	1. when long, like ee in see	ee	**bil**	beel
	2. when short, like i in bit	ih	**mitt**	miht
o	1. when long, like oa in coat	oa	**sko**	sk**oa**
	2. like the exclamation oh	oh	**font**	fohnt
u	1. when long, eu in feud	eu	**ruta**	r**eu**•ta
	2. when short, like u in up	uh	**uppe**	uh•per
y	like ew in new	ew	**byta**	b**ew**•ta
å	1. when long, like oa in oar	oa	**gå**	g**oa**
	2. when short, like o in hot	oh	**åtta**	oh•ta
ä	1. when long, like ai in air	ai	**här**	hair

	2. when short, like e in set	eh	**säng**	sehng
ö	1. when long, like u in cure	ur	**smör**	sm**ur**
	2. when short, like u in nut	uh	**rött**	ruhrt

Swedish vowels are divided into two groups: hard and soft. **A**, **o**, **u** and **å** are hard vowels; **e**, **i**, **y**, **ä** and **ö** are soft vowels. Vowels can also be pronounced either long or short. When a vowel is pronounced "long" the sound is longer, but also more open and rounder. The "short" vowel sounds are more closed, literally a "shorter" sound than a long vowel. An easy rule to remember is that if the vowel is followed by a single consonant, as in **stad** (city), it is long. If the vowel is followed by a double consonant, as in **katt** (cat), the vowel is short. The exception to this rule is with the consonants **m** and **n**.

Swedish is spoken throughout Sweden as well as in the coastal regions of Finland and Estonia. While written Swedish has been standardized, there are characteristic spoken dialects in certain regions such as Gotland, Skåne and Dalarna. Other languages, in addition to Swedish, are also spoken in Sweden, such as Finnish, which is spoken in some communities in Northern Sweden, and the Sámi (Lappish) languages, which are spoken in Sámi communities throughout Northern Norway, Sweden, Finland and Russia. Swedish, Norwegian, Danish, Icelandic and Faroese (spoken on the Faroe Islands) are all derived from Old Norse, the language spoken prior to the Viking Age. Over time, the Scandinavian languages developed from this common language. Danish, Norwegian and Swedish are separate and distinct languages but remain close enough that they are mutually intelligible. The Finnish and Sámi languages belong to a different language family, of which Hungarian also belongs.

How to Use This Book

These essential phrases can also be heard on the audio CD.

Sometimes you see two alternatives in italics, separated by a slash. Choose the one that's right for your situation.

Essential

I'm here on *vacation [holiday]/business.*	**Jag är här på *semester/affärsresa.*** yahg air hair p**oa** *seh•mehs•ter/a•fairs•ree•sa*
I'm going to…	**Jag ska resa till…** yahg skah ree•sa tihl…
I'm staying at a *hotel/youth hostel.*	**Jag bor på *hotell/vandrarhem.*** yahg b**oa**r p**ao** *hoh•tehl/vahnd•rar•hehm*

You May See…

TULL	customs
TAXFRIA VAROR	duty-free goods
VAROR ATT FÖRTULLA	goods to declare

Spectator Sports

When's…?	**När börjar…?** nair b**ur**•yar…
– the basketball game	**– basketbollmatchen** bahs•keht•bohl•ma•shchehn
– the cycling race	**– cykeltävlingen** sew•kehl•taiv•lihng•ehn
– the golf tournament	**– golfspelet** golf•spee•leht
– the soccer [football] game	**– fotbollsmatchen** foat•bohls•ma•shchehn

Words you may see are shown in *You May See* boxes.

Any of the words or phrases preceded by dashes can be plugged into the sentence above.

Swedish phrases appear in red.

Read the simplified pronunciation as if it were English. For more on pronunciation, see page 7.

Relationships

I'm…	**Jag är…** yahg air…
– single	**– ogift** oa·yift
– in a relationship	**– i ett förhållande** ee eht furr·hoal·an·der
– married	**– gift** yihft
– divorced	**– skild** shihld
– separated	**– separerad** seh·pa·ree·rad
I'm a *widow/widower.*	**Jag är *änka/änkling.*** yahg air *ehng·ka/ ehngk·lihng*

▶ For numbers, see page 184.

The arrow indicates a cross reference where you'll find related phrases.

Information boxes contain relevant country, culture and language tips.

Swedes shake hands when greeting someone and when saying goodbye; this holds for meeting new people but is also often the case with colleagues or acquaintances.

You May Hear…

Jag talar bara lite engelska. yahg tah-lar bah-ra lee-ter ehng-ehl-ska	I speak only a little English.
Jag talar inte engelska. yahg tah-lar in-ter ehng-ehl-ska	I don't speak English.

Expressions you may hear are shown in *You May Hear* boxes.

Color-coded side bars identify each section of the book.

Norrtälje
Stockholm
Enköping
Mälaren
Södertälje
Strängnäs
Nynäshamn

▼ Survival

Arrival and Departure

Essential

I'm here on *vacation [holiday]/business.*	**Jag är här på *semester/affärsresa.*** yahg air hair poa *seh•mehs•ter/a•fairs•ree•sa*
I'm going to…	**Jag ska resa till…** yahg skah ree•sa tihl…
I'm staying at a *hotel/youth hostel.*	**Jag bor på *hotell/vandrarhem.*** yahg boar poa *hoh•tehl/vahnd•rar•hehm*

You May Hear…

***Er biljett/Ert pass,* tack.** *eer bihl•yeht/eert pas* tak	Your *ticket/passport,* please.
Vad är syftet med ert besök? vahd air sewf•tet meed ehrt beh•surk	What's the purpose of your visit?
Var bor du? vahr boar deu	Where are you staying?
Hur länge ska du stanna? heur lehng•er skah deu stan•a	How long are you staying?
Vem är du här med? vehm air deu hair meed	Who are you here with?

Passport Control and Customs

I'm just passing through.	**Jag är bara på genomresa.** yahg air bah•ra poa ye•nohm•ree•sa
I would like to declare…	**Jag skulle vilja förtulla…** yahg skuh•ler vihl•ya furr•tuh•la…
I have nothing to declare.	**Jag har inget att förtulla.** yahg hahr ihng•eht at furr•tuh•la

You May Hear...

Har du något att förtulla? hahr deu noa•goht at furr•tuh•la	Anything to declare?
Du måste betala tull för det här. deu mos•ter beh•tah•la tuhl furr dee hair	You must pay duty on this.
Var snäll och öppna den här väskan. vahr snehl ohk urp•na dehn hair vehs•kan	Please open this bag.

You May See...

TULL	customs
TAXFRIA VAROR	duty-free goods
VAROR ATT FÖRTULLA	goods to declare
INGET ATT FÖRTULLA	nothing to declare
PASSKONTROLL	passport control
POLIS	police

Money and Banking

Essential

Where's...?	**Var ligger...?** vahr lih•gehr...
– the ATM	**– bankomaten** bank•oa•mah•tehn
– the bank	**– banken** bank•ehn
– the currency exchange office	**– växelkontoret** vehx•ehl•kohn•toar•eht
What time does the bank *open/close*?	**När *öppnar/stänger* banken?** nair *urp•nahr/stehng•ehr* bank•ehn

I'd like to change *dollars/pounds* into kronor.	**Jag skulle vilja växla *dollar/pund* till kronor.** yahg skuh•ler vihl•ya vehx•la *doh•lar/pund* tihl kroa•nohr
I want to cash some traveler's checks [cheques].	**Jag skulle vilja lösa in några resecheckar.** yahg skuh•ler vihl•ya lur•sa ihn noa•gra ree•seh•sheh•kar

ATM, Bank and Currency Exchange

Can I exchange foreign currency here?	**Kan jag växla pengar här?** kan yahg vehx•la pehng•ar hair
What's the exchange rate?	**Vad är växelkursen?** vahd air vehx•ehl•keur•shehn
How much is the fee?	**Hur mycket är expeditionsavgiften?** heur mew•ker air ehx•peh•dee•shoans•afv•yihf•tehn
I've lost my traveler's checks.	**Jag har tappat mina resecheckar.** yahg hahr ta•pat mee•na ree•seh•sheh•kar
I've lost my card.	**Jag har tappat mitt kort.** yahg hahr ta•pat miht koart
My credit cards have been stolen.	**Mina kreditkort är stulna.** mee•na kreh•deet•koart air steul•na
My card doesn't work.	**Mitt kort fungerar inte.** miht koart fuhn•gee•rar ihn•ter

▶For numbers, see page 184.

You May See...

SÄTT IN KORTET	insert card
AVBESTÄLLA	cancel
RENSA	clear

ENTER	enter
PINKOD	PIN
TA UT	withdraw
KVITTOT	receipt

Cash can be obtained from a **Bankomat** (ATM) with MasterCard, Visa, Eurocard, American Express and other international credit cards or with a debit card. It is also possible to exchange traveler's checks in Sweden. In recent years, it has become quite common for the banks to refer customers with traveler's checks to the nearest **växelkontor** (currency exchange business) such as Forex or X-Change. These businesses are often located near or in points of departure/arrival such as airports or train stations, but can also be found in city centers. Remember to bring your passport with you for identification when you want to exchange money or cash traveler's checks. If you need to visit a bank, be aware that most banks close at 3 p.m., though some are open later one day a week, often on Thursdays.

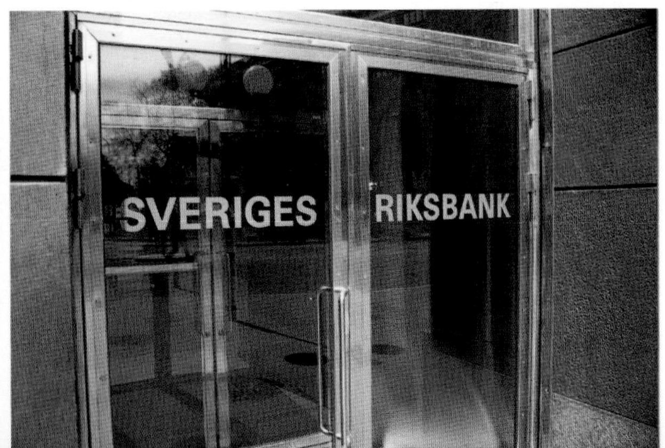

You May See...

Unlike the majority of other European Union countries, Sweden has not adopted the euro as its national currency. Sweden's monetary unit is the **krona** (singular) or **kronor** (plural) abbreviated to **SEK**.

The **krona** is divided into **öre**.

Coins: 50 **öre**, 1 **krona**, 5 and 10 **kronor**

Banknotes: 20, 50, 100, 500 and 1000 **kronor**

Transportation

Essential

How do I get to town?	**Hur kommer jag till staden?** heur koh•mehr yahg tihl stahd•ehn
Where is...?	**Var ligger...?** vahr lih•gehr...
– the airport	**– flygplatsen** flewg•plats•ehn
– the train [railway] station	**– järnvägsstationen** yairn•vehgs•sta•shoa•nehn
– the bus station	**– bussterminalen** bus•tehr•mee•nah•lehn
– the subway [underground] station	**– tunnelbanestationen** teu•nehl•bah•neh•sta•shoan•ehn
How far is it?	**Hur långt är det?** heur loangt air dee
Where can I buy tickets?	**Var kan jag köpa biljetter?** vahr kan yahg chur•pa bil•yeht•tehr
A *one-way [single]/ round-trip [return]* ticket.	**Enkel./Retur.** ehng•kehl/reh•teur
How much does it cost?	**Hur mycket kostar det?** heur mew•ker kos•tar dee
Are there any discounts?	**Finns det några rabatter?** fihns dee noa•gra ra•bat•ehr
Which gate?	**Vid vilken gate?** veed vihl•kehn gayt
Which line?	**Vilken kö?** vihl•kehn kur
Which platform?	**Vilken plattform?** vihl•kehn plat•fohrm
Where can I get a taxi?	**Var kan jag få tag på en taxi?** vahr kan yahg foa tahg poa ehn tax•ee
Please take me to this address.	**Var snäll och kör mig till denna address.** vahr snehl ohk churr may tihl deh•na ad•rehs

Where can I rent a car?	**Var kan jag hyra en bil?** vahr kan yahg hew•ra ehn beel
I'd like a map.	**Jag skulle vilja ha en karta.** yahg skuh•ler vihl•ya h**ah** ehn kahr•ta

Ticketing

When is...to Uppsala?	**När går...till Uppsala?** nair g**oa**r...tihl uhp•sah•la
– the (first) bus	**– (första) bussen** (furs•ta) buhs•ehn
– the (next) flight	**– (nästa) flyg** (nehs•ta) fl**ew**g
– the (last) train	**– (sista) tåget** (sihs•ta) t**oa**•geht
Where can I buy tickets?	**Var kan jag köpa biljetter?** vahr kan yahg ch**ur**•pa bihl•yeht•er
One ticket/Two tickets, please.	***En biljett/Två biljetter*, tack.** *ehn bil•yet/tv**oa** bil•yeht•er* tak
For *today/tomorrow*.	**Till *dagens/imorgon*.** tihl *dah•gens/ee•mo•ron*

▶For days, see page 187.

...ticket.	**...biljett.** ...bihl•yeht
– A one-way [single]	**– En enkel** ehn ehng•kehl
– A round-trip [return]	**– En retur** ehn reh•teur
– A first class	**– En första klass** ehn furr•sta klas
– An economy class	**– En turist klass** ehn tuh•rihst klas
How much does it cost?	**Hur mycket kostar det?** h**eu**r mew•ker kos•tar **dee**
Is there a discount for...?	**Blir det rabatt för...?** bleer d**ee** ra•bat f**u**rr...
– children	**– barn** bahrn
– students	**– studerande** steu•**dee**•ran•der
– senior citizens	**– pensionärer** pan•sh**oa**•nair•ehr

I have an e-ticket.	**Jag har en e-biljett.** yahg hahr ehn ee•bihl•yet
Can I buy a ticket on the *bus/train*?	**Kan jag köpa en biljett på *bussen/ tåget*?** kan yahg chur•pa ehn bihl•yeht poa *bus•ehn/toa•geht*
I'd like to...my reservation.	**Jag skulle vilja...min bokning.** yahg skuh•ler vihl•ya...mihn boak•nihng
– cancel	**– avbeställa** afv•beh•steh•la
– change	**– ändra** ehn•dra
– confirm	**– bekräfta** beh•krehf•ta

Plane

Getting to the Airport

How much is a taxi to the airport?	**Vad kostar en taxi till flygplatsen?** vahd kos•tar ehn tax•ee tihl flewg•plat•sehn
To...Airport, please.	**Till...Flygplats, tack.** tihl...flewg•plats tak
My airline is...	**Mitt flygbolag är...** miht flewg•boa•lahg air...
My flight leaves at...	**Mitt flyg avgår klockan...** miht flewg afv•goar kloh•kan...

▶For time, see page 186.

I'm in a rush.	**Jag har bråttom.** yahg hahr broa•tohm
Can you take an alternate route?	**Kan du köra någon annan väg?** kan deu chur•ra noa•gohn an•nan vehg
Can you drive *faster/ slower*?	**Kan du köra lite *fortare/ långsammare*?** kan deu chur•ra lee•ter *foar•ta•rer/loang•sam•a•rer*

You May Hear...

Vilket flygbolag reser du med? vihl·keht flewg·boa·lahg ree·sehr deu meed	What airline are you flying?
Inrikes eller utrikes? in·ree·kehs ehl·er eut·ree·kehs	Domestic or International?
Vilken terminal? vihl·kehn tehr·mee·nahl	What terminal?

You May See...

ANKOMST	arrivals
AVGÅNG	departures
BAGAGEUTLÄMNING	baggage claim
INRIKESFLYG	domestic flights
UTRIKESFLYG	international flights
CHECKA IN	check-in
CHECKA IN E-BILJETT	e-ticket check-in
AVGÅNGSGATER	departure gates

Check-in and Boarding

Where is check-in?	**Var är incheckningen?** vahr air in·shehk·nihng·ehn
My name is...	**Jag heter...** yahg hee·ter...
I'm going to...	**Jag ska resa till...** yahg skah ree·sa tihl...
How much luggage is allowed?	**Hur mycket gratis bagage får man ha?** heur mew·ker grah·tihs ba·goash foar man hah
Which gate does flight...leave from?	**Vid vilken gate går flygnummer...?** veed vihl·kehn gayt goar flewg·nuhm·ehr...

I'd like *a window/ an aisle* seat.	**Jag skulle vilja ha en *fönsterplats/plats i mittgången.*** yahg skuh·ler vihl·ya hah ehn *furns·tehr·plats/plats ee miht·goang·ehn*
When do we *leave/ arrive*?	**När *avgår vi/är vi framme*?** nair *afv·goar vee/air vee fra·mer*
Is flight...delayed?	**Är det någon försening på flyg...?** air dee noa·gohn furr·seen·ihng poa flewg...
How late will it be?	**Hur försenat är det?** heur furr·seen·at air dee

▶For numbers, see page 184.

You May Hear...

Nästa! nehs·ta	Next!
***Er biljett/Ert pass*, tack.** *eer bihl·yet/eert pas* tak	Your *ticket/passport*, please.
Hur mycket bagage har du? heur mew·ker ba·goash hahr deu	How much luggage do you have?
Du har övervikt. deu hahr ur·vehr·vikt	You have excess luggage.
Det där är *för tungt/för stort* handbagage. dee dair air *furr teungt/furr stoart* hand·ba·goash	That's too *heavy/ large* for a carry-on [to carry on board].
Packade du väskorna själv? pa·ka·der deu vehs·kohr·na shehlv	Did you pack these bags yourself?
Har någon gett er något att ta med? hahr noa·gohn yeht eer noa·goht at tah meed	Did anyone give you anything to carry?
Töm era fickor, tack. turm ee·ra fihk·ohr tak	Empty your pockets, please.
Ta av er skorna, tack. ta afv eer skoar·na tak	Take off your shoes, please.
Nu är ni välkommna att borda flight nummer... neu air nee vail·kohm·na at bohr·da flajt nuhm·ehr...	Now boarding flight...

Luggage

Where *is/are*...?	**Var finns...?** vahr fihns...
– the luggage carts [trolleys]	**– bagagekärrorna** ba·goash·chair·ohr·na
– the luggage lockers	**– förvaringsskåpen** furr·vah·rihng·skoap·ehn
– the baggage claim	**– bagageutlämningen** ba·goash·eut·lehm·nihng·ehn
I've lost my baggage.	**Jag har förlorat mitt bagage.** yahg hahr furr·loa·rat miht ba·goash
My baggage has been stolen.	**Mitt bagage har blivit stulet.** miht ba·goash hahr blee·viht steu·leht
My suitcase was damaged.	**Min resväska blev skadad.** mihn rees·vehs·ka bleev skah·dad

Finding Your Way

Where is...?	**Var finns...?** vahr fihns...
– the currency exchange office	**– växelkontoret** vehx·ehl·kohn·toar·eht
– the car rental [hire]	**– biluthyrningen** beel·eut·hewr·nihng·ehn
– the exit	**– utgången** eut·goang·ehn
– the taxi	**– taxin** tax·een
Is there...into town?	**Finns det...in till stan?** fihns dee...ihn tihl stahn
– a bus	**– en buss** ehn buhs
– a train	**– ett tåg** eht toag
– a subway [underground]	**– tunnelbana** tuh·nehl·bah·na

▶For directions, see page 35.

Train

How do I get to the train station?	**Hur kommer jag till järnvägsstationen?** heur koh·mehr yahg tihl yairn·vaigs·sta·shoa·nehn
How far is it?	**Hur långt är det?** heur loangt air dee
Where *is/are*...?	**Var finns...?** vahr fihns...
– the ticket office	**– biljettkontoret** bihl·yet·kohn·toar·eht
– the luggage lockers	**– förvaringsskåpen** furr·vah·rihng·skoap·ehn
– the platforms	**– plattformarna** plat·fohr·mar·na

▶For directions, see page 35.

▶For ticketing, see page 21.

You May See...

PLATTFORM	platform
SPÅR	tracks
INFORMATION	information
BILJETTKONTOR	ticket office
ANKOMST	arrival
AVGÅNG	departure

Questions

Could I have a schedule [timetable], please?	**Kan jag få en tidtabell, tack?** kan yahg foa ehn teed•ta•behl tak
How long is the trip?	**Hur lång tid tar resan?** heur loang teed tahr ree•san
Do I have to change trains?	**Behöver jag byta tåg?** beh•hur•vehr yahg bew•ta toag

i

Statens järnvägar or **SJ** (The Swedish State Railway) operates an extensive network covering the entire country, while also offering international connections to Olso, Copenhagen and Berlin. The X2000 train, which reaches speed up to 200 km/h, operates to many of Sweden's greater cities and towns. Long-distance trains have restaurant cars and/or buffets, and there are also sleepers and couchettes for both first and second class. The system is reliable and comfortable, and offers a wide range of travel options with respect to schedule and cost. Discount tickets are available for young children, families, students and senior citizens. Special travel cards and programs are also available. On some trains, marked **R** or **IC**, you must reserve a seat by purchasing a **sittplatsbiljett** in addition to your travel ticket. For extraordinary scenery, try the northern **Inlandsbanan** (Inland Railway) service, which runs from Mora in Dalarna to Gällivare beyond the Arctic circle. The **Vildmarksexpressen** (Wilderness Express) has old 1930s coaches and a gourmet restaurant, and runs on the same line between Östersund and Gällivare, with stops and excursions.

▶For useful websites, see page 191.

Departures

When is the train to...?	**När går tåget till...?** nair goar toa·geht tihl...
Is this the right platform for...?	**Är det här rätta plattformen till...?** air dee hair reh·ta plat·fohr·mehn tihl...
Where is platform...?	**Var är plattform...?** vahr air plat·fohrm...
Where do I change for...?	**Var måste jag byta till...?** vahr mos·ter yahg bew·ta tihl...

Boarding

Is this seat taken?	**Är den här platsen upptagen?** air dehn hair plats·ehn uhp·tah·gehn
That's my seat.	**Det där är min plats.** dee dair air mihn plats

You May Hear...

Påstigning! poa·steeg·nihng	All aboard!
Biljetter, tack. bihl·yet·er tak	Tickets, please.
Du måste byta i... deu moss·ter bew·ta ee...	You have to change in...
Nästa hållplats... nehs·ta hoal·plats...	Next stop...

Bus

Where's the bus station?	**Var är bussterminalen?** vahr air bus·tehr·mih·nahl·ehn
How far is it?	**Hur långt är det?** heur loangt air dee
How do I get to...?	**Hur kommer jag till...?** heur koh·mehr yahg tihl...
Does the bus stop at...?	**Stannar bussen vid...?** stan·ar buhs·en veed...

Could you tell me when to get off?	**Kan du tala om för mig när jag ska stiga av?** kan deu tah•la ohm f**u**rr may nair yahg skah stee•ga afv
Do I have to change buses?	**Behöver jag byta buss?** beh•hur•vehr yahg b**ew**•ta buhs
Stop here, please.	**Stanna här, tack.** sta•na hair tak

▶ For ticketing, see page 21.

Public transportation in Sweden is an excellent and well-maintained system that includes **bussar** (buses), **tunnelbanan** (subways), **spårvagnar** (trams) and **tåg** (trains). All of these run frequently, usually between 5 a.m. and midnight on weekdays and a bit later on weekends. Most cities and towns have a bus system, though only a few have trams and subways. While it is possible to purchase single tickets for the different modes of public transportation, it is more cost efficient, not to mention very handy, to purchase a card or set of tickets if you are going to be using a particular network frequently. Most major cities have websites that provide up to date information on routes, tickets and prices; many of the sites have English as a language option.

▶ For useful websites, see page 191.

You May See...

BUSSHÅLLPLATS	bus stop
INGÅNG/UTGÅNG	enter/exit
STÄMPLA ER BILJETT	stamp your ticket

Subway [Underground]

Where's the nearest subway [underground] station?
Var är närmaste tunnelbanestation? vahr air nair•mas•ter tuh•nehl•bah•neh•sta•shoan

Could I have a map of the subway [underground], please?
Kan jag få en tunnelbanekarta, tack? kan yahg foa ehn tuh•nehl•bah•neh•kahr•ta tak

Which line should I take for...?
Vilken linje ska jag ta till...? vihl•kehn leen•yeh skah yahg tah tihl...

Where do I change for...?
Var måste jag byta till...? vahr mos•ter yahg bew•ta tihl...

Is this the train to...?
Är det här tåget till...? air dee hair toa•geht tihl...

Where are we?
Var är vi? vahr air vee

▶For ticketing, see page 21.

The subway in Stockholm is efficient and easy to use. It runs from 5:00 a.m. to midnight on weekdays. Tickets, valid for one hour from the time they are stamped, can be bought from the ticket booths; discount cards can be purchased from **Pressbyrån** (a newsstand). Tickets can also be purchased at SL Centers, some tourist offices and certain grocery stores. The public transportation websites will have information on these retailers and businesses and what types of tickets they sell. Day and multi-day cards are also available. Subway and bus tickets in Stockholm are interchangeable.

Boat and Ferry

When is the car ferry to Gotland leaving?
Hur dags går bilfärjan till Gotland? heur daks goar beel•fair•yan tihl goht•land

Where are the life jackets?
Var finns flytvästarna? vahr fihns flewt•vehs•tar•na

Can I drive on to the ferry now?	**Får jag köra ombord nu?** foar yahg churˑra ohm bohrd neu
How long is the trip?	**Hur lång är resan?** heur loang air reeˑsan
Where should I park?	**Var ska jag parkera?** vahr skah yahg parˑkeeˑra

▶For ticketing, see page 21.

You May See...

LIVBÅT	life boat
FLYTVÄST	life jacket
ACTIVERA HANDBROMSEN	use parking brake
LÄMNA INTE VÄRDESAKER I BILEN	do not leave valuables in your car

Regular boat and ferry services, carrying cars and passengers, link Sweden to neighboring countries such as Norway, Denmark and Germany as well as to the U.K. Ferry services from Stockholm to the vacation destinations of Åland and Gotland in the Baltic Sea are very popular, as are ferries to Finland, Estonia and Latvia. Not to be missed are the ferry and steamer trips from Stockholm to the many surrounding islands, known as **Skärgården** (the Archipelago).

Bicycle and Motorcycle

I'd like to rent [hire]...	**Jag skulle vilja hyra...** yahg skuhˑler vihlˑya hewˑra...
– a bicycle	**– en cykel** ehn sewˑkehl
– a moped	**– en moped** ehn mohˑpeed
– a motorbike	**– en motorcykel** ehn moaˑtohrˑsewˑkehl

How much per *day/ week*?	**Hur mycket kostar det per *dag/ vecka*?** heur mew·ker kos·tar dee pair *dahg/veh·ka*
Can I have a *helmet/ lock*?	**Kan jag få *en hjälm/ett cykelås*?** kan yahg foa *ehn yehlm/eht sew·kehl·loas*

Taxi

Where can I get a taxi?	**Var kan jag få tag på en taxi?** vahr kan yahg foa tahg poa ehn tax·ee
I'd like a taxi *now/for tomorrow* at...	**Jag skulle vilja ha en taxi *nu/imorgon* klockan...** yahg skuh·ler vihl·ya hah ehn tax·ee *neu/ee·mo·ron* kloh·kan...
Pick me up at... (*place/time*)	**Hämta mig *vid/klockan*...** hehm·ta may *veed/kloh·kan*...
I'm going to...	**Jag ska resa till...** yahg skah ree·sa tihl...
– this address	**– denna adress** deh·na ad·rehs
– the airport	**– flygplatsen** flewg·plat·sehn
– the train [railway] station	**– järnvägsstationen** yairn·vaigs·sta·shoa·nehn
I'm late.	**Jag är sen.** yahg air seen
Can you drive *faster/ slower*?	**Kan du köra *fortare/långsammare*?** kan deu chur·ra *fohrt·a·rer/loang·sam·a·rer*
Stop/Wait here.	***Stanna/Vänta* här.** *sta·na/vehn·ta* hair
How much?	**Hur mycket kostar det?** heur mew·ker kos·tar dee
You said it would cost...kronor.	**Du sa att det skulle kosta...kronor.** deu sah at dee skuh·ler kos·ta...kroa·nohr
Keep the change.	**Behåll växeln.** be·hoal vehx·ehln
A receipt, please.	**Kvittot, tack.** kvih·tot tak

▶For numbers, see page 184.

You May Hear...

Vart vill du åka? vart vihl deu oa·ka — Where to?

Vilken adress? vihl·kehn ad·rehs — What's the address?

You can find a taxi at stands marked **Taxi.** You can also flag down a taxi in the street, especially near hotels and bus and train stations. Calling a taxi by phone is a third option; numbers are available from your concierge or a local phone book. The sign **Ledig** (free), when on, indicates that the taxi is available.

Car

Car Rental [Hire]

Where can I rent [hire] a car?	**Var kan jag hyra en bil?** vahr kan yahg hew·ra ehn beel
I'd like to rent [hire]...	**Jag skulle vilja hyra...** yahg skuh·ler vihl·ya hew·ra...
– a *2-/4*-door car	**– en bil med *två/fyra* dörrar** ehn beel meed *tvoa/few·ra* dur·rar
– an automatic car	**– en bil med automatväxel** ehn beel meed ah·toa·maht·vehx·ehl
– a car with air conditioning	**– en bil med luftkonditionering** ehn beel meed luhft·kohn·dee·shoa·neer·ihng
– a car seat	**– en bilbarnstol** ehn beel·barn·stoal
How much does it cost...?	**Hur mycket kostar det...?** heur mew·ker kos·tar dee...
– per *day/week*	**– per *dag/vecka*** pair *dahg/veh·ka*
– per kilometer	**– per kilometer** pair chee·loh·mee·ter

How much does it cost...?	**Hur mycket kostar det...?** heur mew·ker kos·tar dee...
– for unlimited mileage	**– för obegränsade mil** furr oa·beh·grehn·sa·deh·meel
– with insurance	**– med försäkring** meed furr·sair·krihng
Are there any special weekend rates?	**Har ni särskilda helgrabatter?** hahr nee sair·shihl·da hely·ra·bat·ehr

You May Hear...

Har du ett internationellt körkort? hahr deu eht in·tehr·na·shoa·nehlt churr·koart	Do you have an international driver's license?
Kan jag få se ert pass, tack? kan yahg foa see eert pas tak	May I see your passport, please?
Vill du ha en försäkring? vil deu hah ehn furr·sair·krihng	Do you want insurance?
Det blir en handpenning på... dee bleer ehn hand·peh·nihng poa...	There is a deposit of...
Underteckna här, tack. uhn·der·tehk·na hair tak	Please sign here.

Gas [Petrol] Station

Where's the next gas [petrol] station, please?	**Ursäkta, var är närmaste bensinstation?** eur·shehk·ta vahr air nair·mas·teh behn·seen·sta·shoan
Fill it up, please.	**Fyll tanken, tack.** feyl tan·kehn tak
...liters, please.	**...liter, tack.** ...lee·tehr tak
I'll pay *in cash/by credit card.*	**Jag betalar *kontant/med kreditkort.*** yahg beh·tah·lar *kohn·tant/meed kreh·deet·koart*

▶For numbers, see page 184.

You May See...

VANLIG	regular
PREMIUM	premium [super]
DIESEL	diesel

Asking Directions

Is this the road to...?	**Är det här vägen till...?** air dee hair vair•gehn tihl...
How far is it to...?	**Hur långt är det till...?** heur loangt air dee tihl...
Where's...?	**Var ligger...?** vahr lih•gehr...
– ...Street	**– ...gata** ...gah•ta
– this address	**– denna adress** deh•na ad•rehs
– the highway [motorway]	**– motorvägen** moa•tohr•vair•gehn
Can you show me on the map?	**Kan du visa mig på kartan?** kan deu vee•sa may poa kahr•tan
I'm lost.	**Jag har kommit vilse.** yahg hahr koh•miht vihl•ser

You May Hear...

rakt fram rahkt fram	straight ahead
till vänster tihl vehn•stehr	*on/to* the left
till höger tihl hur•gehr	*on/to* the right
***i/runt* hörnan** *ee/ruhnt* hur•nan	*on/around* the corner
mitt emot miht ee•moat	opposite
bakom bah•kohm	behind

bredvid breh·veed	next to
efter ehf·tehr	after
norr/söder nohr/**sur**·dehr	north/south
öster/väster urs·tehr/vehs·tehr	east/west
vid trafikljusen veed tra·feek·**yeus**·ehn	at the traffic light
vid avfarten veed afv·far·tehn	at the exit

You May See...

 **STOPP**	stop
 **LÄMNA FÖRETRÄDE**	yield
 **PARKERING FÖRBJUDEN**	no parking
 **FARLIG KURVA**	dangerous curve
 **ENKELRIKTAT**	one way
 **INGEN INFART**	no entry
 **OMKÖRNING FÖRBJUDEN**	no passing
 **U-SVÄNG FÖRBJUDEN**	no U-turn
ÖVERGÅNGSSTÄLLE FÖR FOTGÄNGARE	pedestrian crossing

Parking

Can I park here?	**Får jag parkera här?** foar yahg par•kee•ra hair
Is there a parking lot [car park] nearby?	**Finns det en parkeringsplats i närheten?** fihns dee ehn par•kee•rihngs•plats ee nair•hee•tehn
How much does it cost...?	**Hur mycket koster det...?** heur mew•ker kos•tar dee...
– per hour	**– per timme** pair tihm•er
– per day	**– per dag** pair dahg
– overnight	**– över natten** ur•vehr na•tehn

Street parking, parking lots and, in some cases, parking garages will be available in most of Sweden's cities and larger towns. Street parking is generally metered in city centers and downtown areas. A blue circular sign with a red slash tells you where parking is prohibited. There will be signs indicating whether or not parking is free. In places where parking is metered, a ticket allowing you to park for a specific period of time will need to be purchased. If this is the case, tickets can be purchased from a **biljettautomat** (ticket machine). You pay for the amount of time you want to park and then place the ticket on the driver's side of the car, on the dashboard, so that the ticket is in plain sight. In some cases, parking may be free, and there will be signs posted with time limits, usually two or three hours.

Breakdown and Repairs

My car *broke down/ won't start.*	**Min bil har *gått sönder/startar inte.*** min beel *hahr goat surn•dehr/star•tar in•ter*
Can you fix it today?	**Kan ni laga den idag?** kan nee lah•ga dehn ee•dahg

When will it be ready?	**När blir den färdig?** nair bleer dehn fair•dihg
How much?	**Hur mycket kostar det?** heur mew•ker kos•tar dee

Accidents

There's been an accident.	**Det har hänt en olycka.** dee hahr hehnt ehn oa•lew•ka
Call *an ambulance/ the police.*	**Ring efter *en ambulans/polisen.*** rihng ehf•ter *ehn am•beu•lans/poa•lee•sehn*

Accommodations

Essential

Can you recommend a hotel in...?	**Kan du rekommendera ett hotel i...?** kan deu reh•koh•mehn•dee•ra eht hoh•tehl ee...
I have a reservation.	**Jag har bokat rum.** yahg hahr boa•kat ruhm
My name is...	**Jag heter...** yahg hee•tehr...
Do you have a room...?	**Har ni ett ledigt rum...?** hahr nee eht lee•dihgt ruhm...
– for *one/two*	**– för *en person/två personer*** furr *ehn pehr•shoan/tvoa pehr•shoan•ehr*
– with a bathroom	**– med badrum** meed bahd•ruhm
– with air conditioning	**– med luftkonditionering** meed luhft•kohn•dee•shoa•neer•ihng
For tonight.	**För ikväll.** furr ee•kvehl
For two nights.	**För två nätter.** furr tvoa neh•tehr
For one week.	**För en vecka.** furr ehn veh•ka
How much?	**Hur mycket kostar det?** heur mew•ker kos•tar dee
Do you have anything cheaper?	**Har ni någonting billigare?** hahr nee noa•gohn•tihng bihl•ee•ga•rer

When's check-out?	**När måste vi checka ut?** nair mos•ter vee sheh•ka eut
Can I leave this in the safe?	**Kan jag lämna detta i kassaskåpet?** kan yahg lehm•na deh•ta ee ka•sah•skoa•peht
Could we leave our baggage here until...?	**Kan vi lämna vårt bagage här till klockan...?** kan vee lehm•na voart ba•goash hair tihl kloh•kan...
Could I have the *bill/receipt*, please?	**Kan jag få *räkningen/kvittot*, tack?** kan yahg foa *rairk•nihng•en/kvih•toht* tak
I'll pay *in cash/by credit card*.	**Jag betalar *kontant/med kreditkort*.** yahg beh•tah•lar *kohn•tant/meed kreh•deet•koart*

Finding Lodging

Can you recommend a hotel in...?	**Kan du rekommendera ett hotel i...?** kan deu reh•koh•mehn•dee•ra eht hoh•tehl ee...
What is it near?	**Vad finns det i närheten?** vahd fihns dee ee nair•hee•tehn
How do I get there?	**Hur kommer jag dit?** heur koh•mehr yahg deet

i

There is a wide range of accommodation in Sweden, from luxury to budget. Budget options include **privatrum** (private rooms), much like bed and breakfasts, or **stugor** (cabins) and **lägenheter** (apartments). Cabins and apartments are usually rented out on a weekly basis, but one- or two-night stays may also be an option. Information can be found at the local tourist office; you may also see signs along the road indicating that there is a vacancy in a cabin nearby. Motorists can look for **motel** (motels); these are reasonably priced with restaurants and car-friendly facilities. When looking for accommodation in university towns such as Stockholm, Göteborg or Lund, staying at a **sommarhotel** (summer hotel) can be a good choice. Student dormitories are open to tourists in the summer and are a good option if you are traveling in a group. Families can enjoy a **familjehotell** (a family hotel), which has special rates for groups sharing the same room (three to six beds). These operate only during the summer months. All-inclusive accommodation is also available in the form of a **turisthotell** (tourist hotel) or **pensionat** (boarding house). These are clean and comfortable hotels or guesthouses that are often found at summer resorts and winter sport areas. Sweden also offers first class and deluxe hotels, usually found in larger cities and towns. Prices and amenities vary but the standards are usually high. Breakfast is usually included. When booking accommodation during the summer months and high tourist season it is important to book in advance.

At the Hotel

I have a reservation.	**Jag har bokat rum.** yahg hahr boh•kat ruhm
My name is…	**Jag heter…** yahg hee•tehr…
Do you have a room…?	**Har ni ett rum…?** hahr nee eht ruhm…
– with a *bathroom [toilet]/shower*	**– med *bad/dusch*** meed *bahd/deush*

– with air conditioning	**– med luftkonditionering** meed luhft•kohn•dee•shoa•neer•ihng
– that's *smoking/ non-smoking*	**– för *rökare/icke-rökare*** furr *rur•kah•rer/ ih•keh rur•ka•rer*
For tonight.	**För ikväll.** furr ee•kvehl
For two nights.	**För två nätter.** furr tvoa neh•tehr
For one week.	**För en vecka.** furr ehn veh•ka

▶For numbers, see page 184.

Does the hotel have...?	**Finns det...på hotellet?** fihns dee...poa hoh•tehl•eht
– a computer	**– en dator** ehn dah•tohr
– an elevator [lift]	**– en hiss** ehn hihs
– (wireless) internet service	**– (trådlös) internet** (troad•lurs) in•tehr•net
– room service	**– rumservice** ruhm•sehr•vihs
– a pool	**– en simbassäng** ehn sihm•ba•sehng
– a gym	**– ett gym** eht ym
I need...	**Jag behöver...** yahg beh•hur•vehr...
– an extra bed	**– en extra säng** ehn ehx•tra sehng
– a cot	**– en tältsäng** ehn tehlt•sehng
– a crib [child's cot]	**– en barnsäng** ehn bahrn•sehng

You May Hear...

Ert *pass/kreditkort*, tack. ehrt *pas/ kreh•deet•koart* tak	Your *passport/credit card*, please.
Kan du fylla i den här blanketten. kan deu few•la ee dehn hair blan•keh•tehn	Please fill out this form.
Skriv under här. skreev uhn•der hair	Sign here.

Price

How much per *night/week*?	**Vad kostar det per *natt/vecka*?** vahd kos·tar d**ee** pair *nat/veh·ka*
Does the price include *breakfast/sales tax [VAT]*?	**Ingår *frukost/moms* i priset?** ihn·g**oa**r *fruh·kohst/mohms* ee pree·seht

Questions

Where's...?	**Var ligger...?** vahr lih·gehr...
– the bar	**– baren** bah·rehn
– the bathroom [toilet]	**– toaletten** toa·ah·leh·tehn
– the elevator [lift]	**– hissen** his·ehn
Can I have...?	**Kan jag få...?** kan yahg f**oa**...
– a blanket	**– ett täcke** eht teh·ker
– an iron	**– ett strykjärn** eht str**ew**k·yairn
– a pillow	**– en kudde** ehn keu·der
– soap	**– tvål** tv**oa**l
– toilet paper	**– toalettpapper** toa·ah·leht·pa·pehr
– a towel	**– en handduk** ehn han·d**eu**k
Can I use this adapter here?	**Kan jag använda den här adaptern här?** kan yahg an·vehn·da dehn hair a·dap·tern hair
How do I turn on the lights?	**Hur tänder man lamporna?** heur tehn·der man lam·pohr·na
Could you wake me at...?	**Kan ni väcka mig klockan...?** kan nee veh·ka may kloh·kan...
Could I have my things from the safe?	**Kan jag få mina saker från kassaskåpet?** kan yahg f**oa** mee·na sah·ker fr**oa**n ka·sa·sk**oa**·peht
Is there *any mail/a message* for me?	**Finns det *någon post/eht meddelande* till mig?** fihns d**ee** *noa·gohn pohst/eht meed·d**ee**l·an·der* tihl may

You May See...

TRYCK	push
DRAG	pull
WC	restroom [toilet]
DAMTOALETT	women's restroom
HERRTOALETT	men's restroom
DUSCH	shower
HISS	elevator [lift]
TRAPPOR	stairs
TVÄTT	laundry
VAR GOD STÖR EJ	do not disturb
BRANDUTGÅNG	fire door
NÖDUTGÅNG	emergency exit
TELEFONVÄCKNING	wake-up call

Problems

There's a problem.	**Jag har ett problem.** yahg hahr eht proh•bleem
I've lost my *key/key card*.	**Jag har tappat bort *min nyckel/mitt nyckelkort*.** yahg hahr ta•pat bort *mihn new•kehl/miht new•kehl•koart*
I've locked myself out of my room.	**Jag har låst ut mig ur rummet.** yahg hahr loast eut may eur ruhm•eht
There's no *hot water/ toilet paper*.	**Det finns inget *varmvatten/ toalettpapper*.** dee fihns ihng•eht *varmt•va•tehrn/toa•ah•leht•pa•per*
The room is dirty.	**Rummet är smutsigt.** ruhm•eht air smuht•siht
There are bugs in our room.	**Det finns insekter på vårt rum.** dee fihns ihn•sehk•tehr poa voart ruhm
...*is/are* broken.	**...är trasig.** ...air trah•sihg

Can you fix...? **Kan ni laga...?** kan nee lah·ga...

– the air conditioning **– luftkonditioneringen** luhft·kohn·dee·shoa·neer·ihng·ehn

– the fan **– fläkten** flehk·tehn

– the heating **– värmen** vair·mehn

– the light **– lampan** lahm·pan

– the TV **– teven** teh·veen

– the toilet **– toaletten** toa·ah·leh·tehn

I'd like to move to another room. **Jag skulle vilja flytta till ett annat rum.** yahg skuh·ler vihl·ya flew·ta tihl eht an·at ruhm

Throughout Sweden the current is 230-volt, 50-cycle AC. If you bring your own electrical appliances, buy a continental adapter plug (round pins) before leaving home. You may also need a transformer appropriate to the wattage of the appliance.

Check-out

When do we need to check out? **När måste vi checka ut?** nair mos·ter vee sheh·ka eut

Could we leave our baggage here until...? **Kan vi lämna vårt bagage här till klockan...?** kan vee lehm·na voart ba·goash hair tihl kloh·kan...

Can I have an itemized *bill/receipt*? **Kan jag få en specificerad *räkning/ett specificerad kvitto*?** kan yahg foa *ehn speh·seh·fee·ee·rad rairk·ning/eht speh·seh·fee·ee·rad kvih·toh*

I think there's a mistake in this bill. **Jag tror det måste vara fel på notan.** yahg troar dee mos·ter vah·ra feel poa noa·tan.

I'll pay *in cash/by credit card*. **Jag betalar *kontant/med kreditkort*.** yahg beh·tah·lar *kohn·tant/meed kreh·deet·koart*

A service charge as well as **moms** (sales tax) is included in hotel and restaurant bills, but you are expected to round up a restaurant bill to the nearest krona. Tipping is generally not expected, but it's always appreciated if the service has been exceptionally good. It is customary to give a small tip to hairdressers, barbers, taxi drivers and porters.

Renting

I've reserved *an apartment/a room*.	**Jag har bokat *en lägenhet/ett rum*.** yahg hahr boh·kat *ehn lair·gehn·heet/eht ruhm*
My name is...	**Jag heter...** yahg hee·tehr...
Can I have the *key/key card*?	**Kan jag få *nyckeln/nyckelkortet*?** kan yahg foa *new·kehln/new·kehl·koar·teht*
Are there...?	**Finns det...?** fihns dee...
– dishes	**– porslin** poarsh·leen
– pillows	**– kuddar** keu·dar
– sheets	**– lakan** lah·kan
– towels	**– handdukar** han·deu·kar
– utensils	**– bestick** beh·stihk
When do I put out the trash [rubbish]?	**När ska jag ställa ut soporna?** nair skah yahg steh·la eut soa·pohr·na
...has broken down.	**...har gått sönder.** ...hahr goat surn·dehr
How does...work?	**Hur fungerar...?** heur fuhn·geh·rar...
– the air conditioner	**– luftkonditioneringen** luhft·kohn·dee·shoa·neer·ihng·ehn
– the dishwasher	**– diskmaskinen** dihsk·ma·shee·nehn
– the freezer	**– frysen** frew·sen
– the heater	**– värmeelementet** vair·meh·ehl·eh·mehn·teht
– the microwave	**– mikrovågsugnen** mik·roh·voags·eung·nehn

How does…work?	**Hur fungerar…?** heur fuhn•geh•rar…
– the refrigerator	**– kylskåpet** kewl•skoa•peht
– the stove	**– spisen** spee•sehn
– the washing machine	**– tvättmaskinen** tveht•mah•shee•nehn

Household Items

I'd like…	**Jag skulle vilja ha…** yahg skuh•ler vihl•ya hah…
– an adapter	**– en adapter** ehn a•dap•tehr
– aluminum kitchen foil	**– aluminiumfolie** ah•leu•mee•nee•um•foh•lyer
– a bottle opener	**– en flasköppnare** ehn flask•urp•na•rer
– a broom	**– en sopborste** ehn sop•borsh•ter
– a can opener	**– en konservöppnare** ehn kohn•serv•urp•na•rer
– cleaning supplies	**– städutrustning** staird•eut•reust•nihng
– a corkscrew	**– en korkskruv** ehn kohrk•skreuv
– detergent	**– tvättmedel** tveht•mee•dehl
– dishwashing liquid	**– diskmedel** disk•mee•dehl
– garbage [rubbish] bags	**– soppåsar** sop•poa•sar
– a light bulb	**– en glödlampa** ehn glurd•lam•pa
– matches	**– tändstickor** tehnd•stih•kohr
– a mop	**– en skurmopp** ehn skewr•mop
– napkins	**– pappersservetter** pa•pers•sahr•veh•ter
– plastic wrap [cling film]	**– plastfolie** plast•foh•lyer
– a plunger	**– en vaskrensare** ehn vask•rehn•sa•rer

– scissors	– **en sax** ehn sax
– a vacuum cleaner	– **en dammsugare** ehn damm•seu•ga•rer

▶For dishes and utensils, see page 68.

▶For oven temperatures, see page 190.

Hostel

Do you have any places left for tonight?	**Finns det några lediga platser ikväll?** fihns dee noa•gra lee•dih•ga plats•ehr ee•kvehl
Can I have...?	**Kan jag få...?** kan yahg foa...
– a *single/double* room	– **ett *enkelrum/dubbelrum*** eht *ehng•kehl•ruhm/duh•behl•ruhm*
– a blanket	– **ett täcke** eht tehk•er
– a pillow	– **en kudde** ehn keu•der
– sheets	– **lakan** lah•kan
– a towel	– **en handduk** ehn han•deuk
What time are the doors locked?	**När stängs ytterdörrarna?** nair stehngs ew•ter•dur•ar•na

If you are looking for something comfortable and reasonably priced, **Svenska Turistföreningen** or **STF** (The Swedish Tourist Club) is an excellent place to start. Here you can search for accommodations such as **vandrarhem** (youth hostels). If you are a member of **STF** or Hostelling International you get a member discount. Generally, room options include dormitory style rooms, split male and female, as well as smaller private rooms or family rooms. You are usually expected to bring your own towels and sheets as these usually are not provided, but can be rented. Shared kitchen facilities are often available, so that you can buy food at the local supermarket and prepare your own meals. Some hostels offer breakfast.

Camping

Can I camp here?	**Får man tälta här?** foar man <u>tehl</u>·ta hair
Is there a campsite near here?	**Finns det en campingplats i närheten?** fihns dee ehn <u>kam</u>·pihng·plats ee <u>nair</u>·hee·tehn
What is the charge per *day/week*?	**Vad kostar det per *dag/vecka?*** vahd <u>kos</u>·tar dee pair *dahg/<u>veh</u>·ka*
Are there...?	**Finns det...?** fihns dee...
– cooking facilities	**– kokmöjligheter** <u>koak</u>·mury·lihg·hee·tehr
– electrical outlets	**– nätuttag** <u>nairt</u>·eut·tahg
– laundry facilities	**– tvättmöjligheter** <u>tveht</u>·mury·lig·hee·tehr
– showers	**– dusch** deush
– tents for rent [hire]	**– tält för uthyrning** tehlt furr <u>eut</u>·hewr·nihng
Where can I empty the chemical toilet?	**– Var kan jag tömma den kemiska toaletten?** vahr kan yahg <u>tur</u>·ma dehn <u>sheh</u>·mihs·ka toa·ah·<u>leh</u>·tehn

You May See...

DRICKSVATTEN	drinking water
INGEN CAMPING	no camping
INGEN GRILLNING	no barbeques
INGEN ÖPPEN ELD	no fires

▶For household items, see page 46.

▶For dishes, utensils and kitchen tools, see page 68.

Internet and Communications

Essential

Where's an internet cafe?	**Var finns det ett internetkafé?** vahr fihns **dee** eht ihn•tehr•neht•ka•feh
Can I access *the internet/check e-mail* here?	**Kan jag *komma ut på internet/kolla e-post* här?** kan yahg *koh•ma eut p***oa** *ihn•tehr•neht /koa•la ee•pohst* hair
How much per *hour/half hour*?	**Hur mycket kostar det per *timme/halvtimme*?** heur mew•ker kos•tar **dee** pair *tihm•er/halv•tihm•er*
How do I log on?	**Hur loggar jag in?** heur loh•gar yag ihn
Can I have a phone card?	**Kan jag få ett telefonkort?** kan yahg foa eht teh•leh•f**oa**n•koart
Can I have your phone number?	**Kan jag få ditt telefonnummer?** kan yahg foa diht teh•leh•f**oa**n•nuhm•ehr
Here's my *number/e-mail address*.	**Här är *mitt nummer/min e-postadress*.** hair air *miht nuhm•ehr/mihn ee•pohst•ad•rehs*
Call me.	**Var snäll och ring mig.** vahr snehl ohk ring may
E-mail me.	**Skicka en e-post till mig.** shih•ka ehn ee•pohst tihl may
Hello. This is...	**Hej. Det här är...** hay **dee** hair air...
I'd like to speak to...	**Jag skulle vilja tala med...** yahg skuh•ler vihl•ya tah•la meed...
Repeat that, please.	**Kan du upprepa det, tack.** kan deu uhp•ree•pa dee tak
I'll be in touch.	**Jag hör av mig snart.** yahg h**ur** afv may snahrt
Goodbye.	**Hej då.** hay doa

Where is the post office?	**Var ligger posten?** vahr lih·gehr pohs·tehn
I'd like to send this to…	**Jag skulle vilja skicka det här till…** yahg skuh·ler vihl·ya shih·ka dee hair tihl…

Computer, Internet and E-mail

Does it have wireless internet?	**Finns det trådlös internet där?** fihns dee troad·lurs ihn·tehr·neht dair
How do I turn the computer *on/off*?	**Hur *sätter jag på/stänger jag av* datorn?** heur *seh·tehr yahg poa/stehng·ehr yahg afv* dah·torn
Can I print?	**Kan jag skriva ut?** kan yahg skree·va eut
How do I…?	**Hur gör man för att…?** heur yurr man furr at…
– connect/disconnect	**– koppla upp/koppla ner** kohp·la uhp/kohp·la nehr
– log *on/off*	**– logga *in/ut*** loh·ga *ihn/eut*
– type this symbol	**– skriva in det här tecknet** skree·va ihn dee hair tehk·neht
What's your e-mail?	**Vad har du för e-postadress?** vahd hahr deu furr ee·pohst·ad·rehs
My e-mail is…	**Min e-postadress är…** mihn ee·pohst·ad·rehs air…

You May See…

STÄNG	close
RADERA	delete
E-POST	e-mail
UTGÅNG	exit

HJÄLP	help
INSTANT MESSENGER	instant messenger
INTERNET	internet
LOGGA IN	login
NYTT MEDDELANDE	new message
AV/PÅ	on/off
ÖPPNA	open
SKRIV UT	print
SPARA	save
SKICKA	send
ANVÄNDARNAMN	username
LÖSENORD	password
TRÅDLÖS INTERNET	wireless internet

Phone

A phone card, please.	**Ett telefonkort, tack.** eht teh•leh•foan•koart tak
How much does it cost?	**Hur mycket kostar det?** heur mew•ker kos•tar dee
My phone doesn't work here.	**Min telefon fungerar inte här.** mihn teh•leh•foan fuhn•geh•rar ihn•ter hair
What's the *area/ country* code for…?	**Vad är *riktnumret/landskoden* till…?** vahd air *rikt•nuhm•reht/lands•koa•dehn* tihl…
What's the number for Information?	**Vilket nummer är det till Nummerbyrån?** vihl•keht nuhm•ehr air dee tihl nuhm•ehr•bew•roan
I'd like the number for…	**Jag skulle vilja ha numret till…** yahg skuh•ler vihl•ya hah nuhm•reht tihl…
Can I have your number?	**Kan jag få ditt telefonnummer?** kan yahg foa diht teh•leh•foan•nuhm•ehr
Here's my number.	**Här är mitt nummer.** hair air miht nuhm•ehr

▶ For numbers, see page 184.

Please call me.	**Var snäll och ring mig.** vahr snehl ohk rihng may
Please text me.	**Var snäll och skicka ett sms till mig.** vahr snehl ohk shih•ka eht ehs•ehm•ehs tihl may
I'll call you.	**Jag ringer dig.** yahg rihng•ehr day
I'll text you.	**Jag skickar ett sms till dig.** yahg shih•kar eht ehs•ehm•ehs tihl day

On the Phone

Hello. This is…	**Hej. Det här är…** hay dee hair air…
I'd like to speak to…	**Jag skulle vilja tala med…** yahg skuh·ler vihl·ya tah·la meed…
Extension…	**Anknytning…** an·knewt·nihng…
Speak *louder/more slowly*.	**Var snäll och tala *högre/långsammare*.** vahr snehl ohk tah·la *hur·greh/loang·sam·a·rer*
Can you repeat that?	**Kan du upprepa det?** kan deu uhp·ree·pa dee
I'll call back later.	**Jag ringer senare.** yahg rihng·ehr see·na·rer
Goodbye.	**Hej då.** hay doa

▶ For business travel, see page 160.

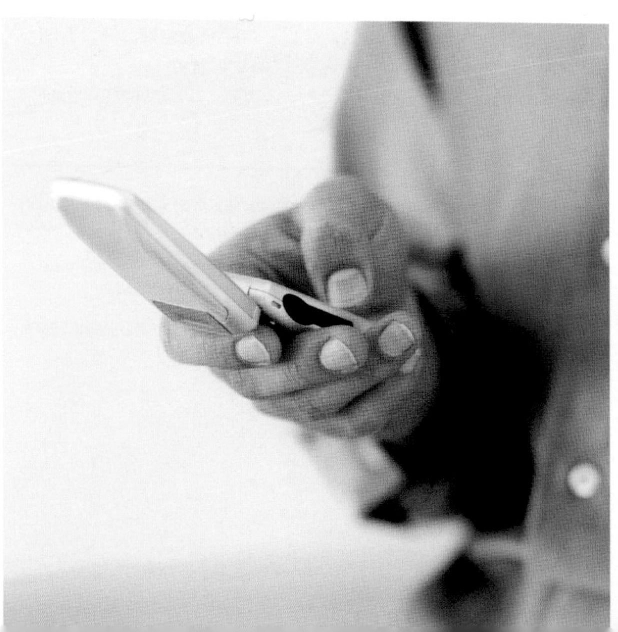

You May Hear...

Vem är det? vehm air dee	Who's calling?
Ett ögonblick. eht ur·gohn·blihk	One moment.
Tyvärr, är *han/hon* inte här. tew·vair air *hahn/hoan* ihn·ter hair	I'm afraid *he/she* is not in.
***Han/Hon* kan inte komma till telefonen.** *hahn/hoan* kan ihn·ter koh·ma tihl teh·leh·foan·ehn	*He/She* can't come to the phone.
Vill du lämna ett meddelande? vihl deu lehm·na eht mee·dee·lan·der	Would you like to leave a message?
Ring tillbaka *senare/om tio minuter.* rihng tihl·bah·ka *see·na·rer/ohm tee·oah mih·neu·tehr*	Call back *later/in 10 minutes.*
Kan *han/hon* ringa upp dig? kan *hahn/hoan* rihng·a uhp day	Can *he/she* call you back?
Vad är ditt telefonnummer? vahd air diht teh·leh·foan·nuhm·ehr	What's your number?

Fax

Can I *send/receive* a fax here? **Kan man *skicka/ta emot* fax här?** kan man *shih·ka/ta ee·moat* fax hair

What's the fax number? **Vad är ditt faxnummer?** vahd air diht fax·nuhm·ehr

Please fax this to... **Var snäll och faxa det här till...** vahr snehl ohk fax·ah dee hair tihl...

Public phones take either **telefonkort** (phone cards) or **kreditkort** (credit cards). Phone cards are available at **Pressbyrån** (newsstand chain) and sometimes at independent newsstands. You can purchase a cell phone with a prepaid SIM card, something which is relatively cost efficient and worthwhile if you will be in Sweden for a longer period. Phone cards can also be used when dialing from any landline, e.g. at home of a friend or from a hotel. To call the U.S. or Canada from Sweden, dial 00 + 1 + area code + phone number. To call the U.K., dial 00 + 44 + area code (minus first 0) + phone number. Information on area codes for Sweden and international dialing codes can be found in the phone book and are usually available at hotels and youth hostels. The emergency number in Sweden is 112.

Post Office

Where's *the post office/mailbox [postbox]*?	**Var ligger *posten/postlådan*?** vahr lih•gehr *pohs•tehn/pohst•loa•dan*
A stamp for this *postcard/letter*, please.	**Kan jag få ett frimärke till det här *vykortet/brevet*, tack.** kan yahg f**oa** eht free•mair•ker tihl d**ee** hair *vew•koar•teht/ bree•veht* tak
How much does it cost?	**Hur mycket kostar det?** heur mew•ker kos•tar d**ee**
I want to send this package *by airmail/ express.*	**Jag vill skicka det här paketet *med flygpost/express.*** yahg vihl shih•ka d**ee** hair pa•kee•teht meed *flewg•pohst/ehx•prehs*
The receipt, please.	**Kvittot, tack.** kvih•toht tak

You May Hear…

Fyll i tulldeklarationen, tack. fewl ee tuhl·deh·klar·a·shoa·nehn tak	Please fill out the customs declaration form.
Vad är värdet? vahd air vair·deht	What's the value?
Vad finns inuti? vahd fihns ihn·eu·tee	What's inside?

Posten (the post office) is easy to find, just look for the blue **Post** sign with a yellow horn. Mailboxes are bright yellow. Business hours are 9 a.m. to 6 p.m. and until 1 p.m. on Saturdays. Like many other stores and business, you will need to take a number and wait for it to be called or displayed on a screen before you can be helped. Stamps can be purchased at **Pressbyrån** (newsstand chain) as well as some grocery stores.

▼ Food

Eating Out

Essential

Can you recommend a good *restaurant/bar*?	**Kan du rekommendera en bra *restaurang/pub?*** kan deu reh•koh•mehn•dee•ra ehn brah *rehs•teu•rang/peub*
Is there *a traditional Swedish/an inexpensive* restaurant nearby?	**Finns det *något värdshus/någon billigare restaurang* i närheten?** fihns dee *noa•goht vairds•heus/noa•gohn bihl•ih•ga•rer rehs•teu•rang* ee nair•hee•tehn
A table for…, please.	**Ett bord för…, tack.** eht bohrd furr…tak
Could we sit…?	**Får vi sitta…?** foar vee siht•a…
– here/there	**– här/där** hair/dair
– outside	**– ute** eu•ter
– in a non-smoking area	**– vid bord för icke-rökare** veed bohrd furr ee•keh•rur•ka•rer
I'm waiting for someone.	**Jag väntar på någon.** yahg vairn•tar poa noa•gohn
Where are the restrooms [toilets]?	**Var finns toaletten?** vahr fihns toa•ah•leh•tehn
A menu, please.	**En meny, tack.** ehn meh•neu tak
What do you recommend?	**Vad rekommenderar du?** vahd reh•koh•mehn•dee•rar deu
I'd like…	**Jag skulle vilja ha…** yahg skuh•ler vihl•ya hah…
Some more…, please.	**Lite mer…, tack.** lee•ter meer…tak
Enjoy your meal.	**Smaklig måltid.** smahk•lihg moal•teed
The check [bill], please.	**Kan jag få räkningen, tack.** kan yahg foa rairk•nihng•ehn tak

Is service included?	**Är serveringsavgiften inräknad?** air ser•veeh•rihngs•afv•yihf•tehn ihn•rairk•nad
Can I pay by credit card?	**Kan jag betala med kreditkort?** kan yahg beh•tah•la meed kreh•deet•koart
Can I have the receipt, please?	**Kan jag få kvittot, tack?** kan yahg f**oa** kvih•toht tak
Thank you.	**Tack.** tak

Restaurant Types

Can you recommend…?	**Kan du rekommendera…?** kan deu reh•koh•mehn•dee•ra…
– a restaurant	**– en restaurang** ehn rehs•teu•rang
– a bar	**– en bar** ehn bahr
– a cafe	**– ett kafé** eht ka•feh
– a fast-food place	**– en grillbar** ehn grihl•bahr
– a steakhouse	**– ett stekhus** eht steek•heus

When it comes to eating out, there are many options, ranging from fast-food stands to five-star restaurants. If you are looking for a quick bite to eat, then a **gatukök** (fast-food stand) is an easy choice. If you are looking for more traditional cuisine, this can be found at a **värdshus** (roadside restaurant), **kafé** (cafe) or **restaurang** (restaurant).

Reservations and Questions

I'd like to reserve a table…	**Jag skulle vilja boka ett bord…** yahg skuh•ler vihl•ya boh•ka eht bohrd…
– for two	**– för två** furr tv**oa**
– for this evening	**– till ikväll** tihl ee•kvehl
– for tomorrow at…	**– imorgon klockan…** ee•mo•ron kloh•kan…

A table for two, please.	**Kan jag få ett bord för två tack.** kan yahg foa eht bohrd furr tvoa tak
We have a reservation.	**Vi har bokat ett bord.** vee hahr boa•kat eht bohrd
My name is…	**Jag heter…** yahg hee•tehr…
Could we sit…?	**Får vi sitta…?** foar vee siht•a…
– here/there	**– här/där** hair/dair
– outside	**– ute** eu•ter
– in a non-smoking area	**– vid bord för icke-rökare** veed bohrd furr ee•keh•rur•kah•rer
– by the window	**– vid fönstret** veed furns•treht
Where are the restrooms [toilets]?	**Var finns toaletten?** vahr fihns toa•ah•leh•tehn

You May Hear…

Har ni bokat? hahr nee boh•kat	Do you have a reservation?
Hur många blir ni? heur moang•a bleer nee	How many?
Rökare eller icke-rökare? rur•ka•rer ehl•ehr ee•keh•rur•ka•rer	Smoking or non-smoking?
Vill ni beställa? vihl nee beh•steh•la	Are you ready to order?
Vad vill ni beställa? vahd vihl nee beh•steh•la	What would you like?
Jag kan rekommendera… yahg kan reh•koh•mehn•dee•ra…	I recommend…
Smaklig måltid. smahk•lihg moal•teed	Enjoy your meal.

Ordering

Excuse me!	**Ursäkta!** eur·shehk·ta
We're ready to order.	**Vi vill gärna beställa.** vee vihl yair·na beh·steh·la
May I see the wine list?	**Kan jag få se vinlistan?** kan yahg foa see veen·lihs·tan
I'd like…	**Jag skulle vilja ha…** yahg skuh·ler vihl·ya hah…
– a bottle of…	**– en flaska…** ehn flahs·ka…
– a glass of…	**– ett glas…** eht glahs…
– a carafe of…	**– en karaff…** ehn kah·raf…

▶For alcoholic and non-alcoholic drinks, see page 90.

The menu, please.	**En meny, tack.** ehn meh·neu tak
Do you have…?	**Har ni…?** hahr nee…
– a menu in English	**– en meny på engelska** ehn meh·neu poa ehng·ehl·ska
– a fixed price menu	**– en meny med fast pris** ehn meh·neu meed fast prees
– a children's menu	**– en barnmeny** ehn bahrn·meh·neu

What do you recommend?	**Vad rekommenderar ni?** vahd reh•koh•mehn•dee•rar nee
What's this?	**Vad är det här?** vahd air d**ee** hair
What's in it?	**Vad är det i den?** vahd air d**ee** ee dehn
Is it spicy?	**Är den kryddstark?** air dehn kreyd•stark
It's to go [take away].	**Jag ska ta den med mig.** yahg skah tah dehn meed may

You May See...

KUVERTAVGIFT	cover charge
FAST PRIS	fixed-price
MENY	menu
DAGENS MENY	menu of the day
DRICKS (INTE) INRÄKNAD	service (not) included
SPECIALITETER	specials

Cooking Methods

baked	**bakad** bah•kad
boiled	**kokt** koakt
braised	**bräserad** braeh•seeh•rad
breaded	**panerad** pah•neeh•rad
creamed	**rörd** rurd
diced	**i bitar** ee bee•tar
fileted	**filead** fih•leeh•ad
fried	**stekt** steekt

grilled	**grillad** grihl•ad
poached	**pocherad** poa•sheeh•rad
roasted	**ugnstekt** eungn•steekt
sautéed	**stekt** steekt
smoked	**rökt** rurkt
steamed	**ångkokt** oang•koakt
stewed	**stuvad** steu•vad
stuffed	**fylld** fewld

Special Requirements

I am…	**Jag är…** yahg air…
– diabetic	**– diabetiker** dee•a•beh•tih•ker
– lactose intolerant	**– laktosintolerant** lak•toas•in•toh•leh•rant
– vegetarian	**– vegetarian** veh•geh•ta•ree•ahn
I'm allergic to…	**Jag är allergisk mot…** yahg air a•lehr•gihsk moat…
I can't eat food that contains…	**Jag kan inte äta mat som innehåller…** yahg kan ihn•ter air•ta maht som ihn•neh•hoa•lehr…
– dairy	**– mejeriprodukter** may•eh•ree•proh•duhk•tehr
– gluten	**– gluten** glue•tehn
– nut	**– nöt** nurt
– pork	**– fläskkött** flehsk•churt
– shellfish	**– skaldjur** skahl•yeur
– spicy food	**– kryddad mat** krew•dad maht
– wheat	**– vete** veeh•te

Dining with Kids

Do you have a children's menu?	**Har ni en barnmeny?** hahr nee ehn bahrn·meh·neu
Can you bring a high chair, please?	**Kan jag få en barnstol, tack?** kan yahg foa ehn bahrn·stoa/ tak
Where can I *feed/ change* the baby?	**Var kan jag *mata/byta på* babyn?** vahr kan yahg *mah·ta/bew·ta poa* bai·been
Can you warm this?	**Kan ni värma det här?** kan nee vair·ma dee hair

▶ For travel with children, see page 162.

Complaints

How much longer will our food be?	**Hur länge till behöver vi vänta?** heur lehng·er tihl beh·hur·ver vee vehn·ta
We can't wait any longer.	**Vi kan inte vänta längre.** vee kan ihn·ter vehn·ta lehng·rer
We're leaving.	**Vi går nu.** vee goar neu
That's not what I ordered.	**Det här har jag inte beställt.** dee hair hahr yahg ihn·ter beh·stehlt
I asked for…	**Jag beställde…** yahg beh·stehl·der…
I can't eat this.	**Jag kan inte äta det här.** yahg kan ihn·ter air·ta dee hair
This is too…	**Det här är för…** dee hair air furr…
– cold/hot	**– kallt/varmt** kalt/varmt
– salty/spicy	**– salt/kryddat** salt/krew·dat
– tough/bland	**– segt/smaklöst** sekt/smahk·lurst
This isn't *clean/fresh*.	**Det här är inte *rent/färskt*.** dee hair air ihn·ter *reent/fairskt*

Paying

The check [bill], please.	**Kan jag få räkningen, tack.** kan yahg f**oa** rairk•nihng•ehn tak
We'd like to pay separately.	**Vi vill betala var för sig.** vee vihl beh•tah•la vahr f**ur**r say
It's all together.	**Allt tillsammans.** alt tihl•saa•mans
Is service included?	**Är serveringsavgiften inräknad?** air sehr•veeh•rihngs•afv•yihf•ten ihn•rairk•nad
What's this amount for?	**Vad står den här summan för?** vahd st**oa**r dehn hair suhm•an f**ur**r
I didn't have that. I had…	**Jag åt inte det. Jag åt…** yahg **oa**t ihn•ter d**ee** yahg **oa**t…
Can I pay by credit card?	**Kan jag betala med kreditkort?** kan yahg beh•tah•la meed kreh•deet•koart
Can I have *an itemized bill/a receipt*?	**Kan jag få *en specificerad räkning/ett kvitto*?** kan yahg f**oa** *ehn speh•seh•fee•ee•rad rairk•nihng/eht kvih•toh*
That was a very good meal.	**Det var en mycket god måltid.** d**ee** vahr ehn mew•ker goad m**oa**l•teed

Market

Where are *the carts [trolleys]/baskets*?	**Var finns *shoppingvagnarna/shoppingkorgarna*?** vahr fihns *shoh•pihng•vagn•nar•na/shoh•pihng•kohr•yar•na*
Where *is/are*…?	**Var finns…?** vahr fihns…

▶For food items, see page 95.

I'd like some of *this/that.*	**Jag skulle vilja ha lite av *det här/det där.*** yahg skuh•ler vihl•ya hah lee•teh afv *d**ee** hair/d**ee** dair*
Can I taste it?	**Får jag smaka?** f**oa**r yahg smah•ka

I'd like…	**Jag skulle vilja ha…** yahg skuh•ler vihl•ya hah…
– a *kilo/half-kilo* of…	**– ett *kilo/halvt kilo*…** eht *chee•loh/halft chee•loh*…
– a *liter/half-liter* of…	**– en *liter/halv liter*…** ehn *lee•ter/halv lee•ter*…
– a piece of…	**– en bit av…** ehn beet afv…
– a slice of…	**– en skiva av…** ehn shee•va afv…
More/Less than that.	***Mer/Mindre* än det där.** *meer/mihn•dreh* ehn dee dair
How much does it cost?	**Hur mycket kostar det?** heur mew•ker kos•tar dee
Where do I pay?	**Var kan jag betala?** vahr kan yahg beh•tah•la
Can I have a bag?	**Kan jag få en påse?** kan yahg foa ehn poa•seh
I'm being helped.	**Tack, jag har fått hjälp.** tak yahg hahr foat yehlp

▶ For conversion tables, see page 190.

You May Hear…

Kan jag hjälpa er? kan yahg yehl•pa eer	Can I help you?
Vad vill ni beställa? vahd vihl nee beh•steh•la	What would you like?
Något annat? noa•goht an•nat	Anything else?
Det kostar…kronor. dee kos•tar…kroa•nohr	That's…kronor.

Although Sweden still has many small, specialty shops, they are slowly giving way to **köpcentrum** (shopping centers), especially in larger towns. You can still find markets that sell fresh fruit and vegetables as well as flowers and some handicrafts. **Julmarknaden** (the traditional Christmas market) in Stockholm is reminiscent of times gone by.

Supermarkets can be found in most large towns, cities and suburbs. **Närbutiker** (corner shops), as well as **Pressbyrån** (newsstand chain) sell a good range of food. In Stockholm, **Östermalmshallen** and **Hötorgshallen** (market halls) sell fresh meat—including reindeer and moose—fish and poultry.

Swedes enjoy a variety of fish and seafood, and one will find a good selection in most restaurants and supermarkets. If you visit Sweden in August, you will no doubt enjoy a **kräftkalas** (crayfish party). There is not much meat on a crayfish, but when helped down with a few glasses of **akvavit** (aquavit) and some salad and cheese, it makes for an unforgettable evening.

You May See...

FÖRBRUKAS FÖRE...	best if used by...
KALORIER	calories
FETTFRI	fat free
MÅSTE FÖRVARAS I KYLSKÅP	keep refrigerated
KAN INNEHÅLLA SPÅR AV...	may contain traces of...
BÄST FÖRE...	sell by...
LÄMPLIGT FÖR VEGETARIANER	suitable for vegetarians

Dishes, Utensils and Kitchen Tools

bottle opener	**flasköppnare** flask•eup•na•rehr
bowl	**djup tallrik** yeup tal•rihk
can opener	**konservöppnare** kohn•sehrv•urp•nah•rer
corkscrew	**korkskruv** kohrk•skreuv
cup	**kopp** kohp
fork	**gaffel** gahf•ehl
frying pan	**stekpanna** steek•pan•na
glass	**glas** glahs
knife	**kniv** kneev
measuring *cup/ spoon*	***mått/måttsked*** *moat/moat•sheed*
napkin	**servett** sehr•vehtt
plate	**tallrik** tal•rihk
pot	**gryta** grew•ta
saucepan	**kastrull** kas•truhl
spatula	**steekspade** steek•spah•der
spoon	**sked** sheed

Meals

Frukost (breakfast) is usually served from 7 to 10 a.m. Hotels and guesthouses offer a large buffet selection of cheese, cold meat, bread, eggs, cereals and **filmjölk** (thick yogurt). **Lunch** (lunch) is served from as early as 11 a.m. Although many Swedes have a warm meal at lunchtime, some opt for a sandwich or a salad. This is the best time to try the **dagens rätt** (specialty of the day). **Middag** (dinner) is normally eaten early, around 6 or 7 p.m., though many restaurants continue serving until late, especially on the weekend. Many Swedes will also eat a meal later in the evening, referred to as **kvällsmål**; this evening meal usually includes sandwiches, yogurt or soup.

Breakfast

apelsin a•pehl•seen	orange
bacon bay•kohn	bacon
bröd brurd	bread
filmjölk feel•myurlk	thick yogurt
frukostflingor fruh•kohst•flihng•or	(cold) cereal
fruktjuice fruhkt•yoas	fruit juice
grapefrukt grape•fruhkt	grapefruit
gröt grurt	(hot) cereal
havregryn hafv•reh•greun	oatmeal
honung hoa•neung	honey
kaffe… ka•fer…	coffee…
– med mjölk meed myurlk	– with milk
– med socker meed soh•ker	– with sugar
– med sötningsmedel meed surt•nihngs•mee•dehl	– with artificial sweetener
– utan koffein eu•tan koh•feen	– decaf
kallskuret kal•skeu•reht	cold cuts [charcuterie]
kokt ägg koakt ehg	boiled egg

I'd like…	**Jag skulle vilja ha…** yahg skuh•ler vihl•ya hah…
More…, please.	**Lite mer…, tack.** lee•teh meer…tak

korv kohrv	sausage
marmelad mar•meh•lahd	marmalade
mjölk myurlk	milk
muffin muh•fihn	muffin
müsli mews•lee	granola [muesli]
omelett ohm•eh•leht	omelet
ost oast	cheese
rostat bröd roahs•tat brurd	toast
småbröd smoa•brurd	roll
smör smur	butter
stekt ägg steekt ehg	fried egg
sylt sewlt	jam
thé tee	tea
vatten va•tehrn	water
yoghurt yoh•geurt	yogurt
ägg ehg	egg
äggröra ehg•rur•ra	scrambled eggs
äpple ehp•leh	apple

Appetizers [Starters]

färska räkor fair•ska rair•kohr	unshelled shrimp [prawns], served with toast, butter and mayonnaise
förrätt furr•reht	appetizer [starter]

With/Without...	**Med/Utan...** meed/eu•tan...
I can't have...	**Jag kan inte äta mat som innehåller...** yahg kan ihn•ter air•ta maht som ih•neh•hoal•lehr...

gravlax grafv•lax	marinated salmon
löjrom lurj•rohm	bleak roe, served with chopped, raw onions and sour cream and eaten on toast
rökt lax **rur**kt lax	smoked salmon
sill sihl	marinated herring
sillbricka sihl•brih•ka	variety of marinated herring
S.O.S. (smör, ost och sill) ehs oa ehs (sm**ur** oast ohk sil)	a small plate of marinated herring, bread, butter and cheese
toast skagen toast skah•gehn	toast with chopped shrimp [prawns] in mayonnaise, topped with bleak roe
viltpastej vihlt•pa•stay	game pâté

Soup

buljong beul•yong	broth
fisksoppa fihsk•sop•a	fish soup
grönsakssoppa gr**ur**n•sa**h**ks•sohp•a	vegetable soup
kall soppa kal sohp•a	cold soup
kycklingsoppa chewk•lihng•sohp•a	chicken soup
kött och grönsakssoppa churt•oa•gr**ur**n•sahk•sohp•a	meat and vegetable soup

I'd like…	**Jag skulle vilja ha…** yahg skuh•ler vihl•ya hah…
More…, please.	**Lite mer…, tack.** lee•teh meer…tak

Meals

köttsoppa churt·sohp·a — a hearty soup of beef, vegetables and dumplings

löksoppa lurk·sohp·a — onion soup

nyponsoppa new·pohn·sohp·a — rose-hip soup

oxsvanssoppa oax·svans·sohp·a — oxtail soup

potatissoppa poa·tah·tihs·sohp·a — potato soup

rörd soppa rurrd sohp·a — cream soup

sparrissoppa spa·rihs·sohp·a — asparagus soup

spenatsoppa speh·nat·sohp·a — a rich soup made from spinach, potatoes, milk and cream

tomatsoppa toa·maht·soh·pa — tomato soup

ärtsoppa airt·sohp·a — green or yellow pea soup

Fish and Seafood

abborre ah·bohr·er — perch

ansjovis an·shoa·vees — anchovy

blåmussla bloa·muhs·la — blue mussel

braxen brak·sehn — sea bream

böckling burk·lihng — smoked Baltic herring

fisk fihsk — fish

forell foa·rehl — trout

färska räkor fairs·ka rair·kohr — unshelled shrimp [prawns]

With/Without...	**Med/Utan...** meed/eu·tan...
I can't have...	**Jag kan inte äta mat som innehåller...** yahg kan ihn·ter air·ta maht som ih·neh·hoal·lehr...

gravlax grafv·lax	marinated salmon
gädda yeh·da	sea perch
halstrad fisk hal·strahd fihsk	grilled fish
halstrad forell med färskpotatis hal·strad foa·rehl med fairsk·poa·tah·tihs	grilled trout with new potatoes
havsabborre hafs·a·boh·rer	sea bass
hummer huhm·ehr	lobster
hälleflundra heh·leh·fleun·dra	halibut
inlagd sill ihn·lagd sil	marinated (pickled) herring
kammussla kam·muhs·la	scallop
kolja kohl·ya	haddock
krabba kra·ba	crab
kräfta krehf·ta	crayfish
kummel keu·mel	hake
lax lax	salmon
löjrom lury·rohm	bleak roe with chopped, raw onions and sour cream; served on toast
makrill mak·rihl	mackerel
marulk mahr·eulk	monkfish
matjesill ma·shcheh·sihl	marinated herring
multe muhl·ter	mullet
mussla muhs·la	mussel

I'd like…	**Jag skulle vilja ha…** yahg skuh·ler vihl·ya hah…
More…, please.	**Lite mer…, tack.** lee·teh meer…tak

mört murt	roach (type of fish)
ostron oas·tron	oyster
piggvar pihg·vahr	turbot
rimmad lax med stuvad potatis rihm·ahd lax meed steu·vad poa·tah·tihs	lightly salted salmon with creamed potatoes and dill
rocka roh·ka	ray (type of fish)
räkor rair·kohr	shrimp [prawns]
röding rur·dihng	char
rödspätta rurd·speh·ta	plaice
rökt fisk rurkt fisk	smoked fish
rökt lax rurkt lax	smoked salmon
rökt ål rurkt oal	smoked eel
sardin sar·deen	sardine
sill sihl	herring
sillbricka sihl·brih·ka	variety of marinated herring
sillsallad sihl·sal·ad	beet and herring salad
sjötunga sjur·tuhng·a	sole
skaldjur skahl·yeur	shellfish
skaldjurssallad skahl·yeurs·sal·ad	shellfish salad
skarpsill skarp·sihl	herring
småsill smoa·sihl	herring

With/Without…	**Med/Utan…** meed/eu·tan…
I can't have…	**Jag kan inte äta mat som innehåller…** yahg kan ihn·ter air·ta maht som ih·neh·hoal·lehr…

S.O.S. (smör, ost och sill) ehs oa ehs (smur oast ohk sihl)	small plate of marinated herring, bread, butter and cheese
stekt fisk steekt fisk	fried fish
strömming struhrm•ihng	sprats (small Baltic herring) filleted and sandwiched in pairs with dill and butter in the middle
strömmingsflundra strurm•ihngs•fleun•dra	Baltic herring, filleted and sandwiched in pairs, fried, with dill and butter filling
stuvad abborre steu•vad a•boh•rer	perch poached with onion, parsley and lemon
tonfisk toan•fihsk	tuna
torsk tohrshk	cod
ugnsbakad fisk eungns•bah•kad fihsk	oven-baked fish
vitling veet•lihng	whiting
ål oal	eel
ångkokt fisk oang•koakt fisk	steamed fish

Meat and Poultry

anka ang•ka	duck
bacon bay•kon	bacon
biffkött bihf•churt	beef

I'd like…	**Jag skulle vilja ha…** yahg skuh•ler vihl•ya hah…
More…, please.	**Lite mer…, tack.** lee•teh meer…tak

biffstek bihf·steek — steak

bog boag — shoulder (cut of meat)

broiler broy·lehr — spring chicken

entrecote an·treh·koat — sirloin steak

falukorv fah·leu·kohrv — lightly spiced sausage

fasan fa·sahn — pheasant

filé fih·leh — filet mignon

fläsk flehsk — pork

fläskben flehsk·been — ham bone

fläskfilé flehsk·fih·leh — fillet of pork

fläskkarré flehsk·ka·reh — pork loin

fläskkorv flehsk·kohrv — spicy, boiled pork sausage

fläsklägg flehsk·lehg — knuckle of pork

fågel foa·gehl — poultry

får foar — mutton

get yeet — kid (goat)

grillad kyckling grihl·ahd chewk·lihng — grilled chicken

gås goas — goose

hamburgare ham·beur·ya·rer — hamburger

hare hah·rer — rabbit

hjort yohrt — deer

isterband ihs·tehr·band — sausage of pork, barley and beef

kalkon kal·koan — turkey

With/Without…	**Med/Utan…** meed/eu·tan…
I can't have…	**Jag kan inte äta mat som innehåller…** yahg kan ihn·ter air·ta maht som ih·neh·hoal·lehr…

kallskuret kal·skeu·reht — cold cuts [charcuterie]

kalops ka·lohps — beef stew

kalvkött kalv·churt — veal

kalvsylta kalv·sewl·ta — cold veal in jelly

karré ka·reh — tenderloin

kokt skinka koakt shihng·ka — boiled ham

korv kohrv — sausage

kotlett koht·lehtt — cutlet

kyckling chewk·lihng — chicken

kycklingbröst chewk·lihng·brurst — chicken breast

kycklinglever chewk·lihng·lee·vehr — chicken liver

kåldomar med gräddsås och lingon koal·dohl·mar meed grehd·soas ohk lihng·ohn — chopped [minced] meat and rice stuffed in cabbage leaves

kött churt — meat

köttbulle churt·buh·ler — meatball

köttfärs churt·fairs — chopped [minced] beef

lamm lamm — lamb

lammgryta lamm·grew·ta — lamb stew

lever lee·vehr — liver

leverpastej lee·vehr pa·stay — liver pâté

lägg lehg — shank (top of leg)

lövbiff lurv·bihf — fried, thinly sliced beef, with onions

I'd like…	**Jag skulle vilja ha…** yahg skuh·ler vihl·ya hah…
More…, please.	**Lite mer…, tack.** lee·teh meer…tak

medaljong meh·dal·yong	small fillet of cut meat
njure nyeu·rer	kidney
nötkött nurt·churt	red meat
oxkött oax·churt	ox
oxrullad oax·reu·lahd	braised roll of beef
oxsvans oax·svans	oxtail
pannbiff pan·bihf	beef patty
prinskorv prihns·kohrv	small pork sausage
pärlhöns pairl·hurns	guinea fowl
ragu ra·guh	beef stew
rapphöna rap·hurna	partridge
ren reen	reindeer
renstek med svampsås reen·steek meed svamp·soas	roast reindeer with mushroom sauce
revbensspjäll reev·beens·spehl	spareribs
rostbiff rohst·bihf	roast beef
rumpstek ruhmp·steek	rump steak
rådjur roa·yeur	venison
rådjursstek roa·yeur·steek	roast of venison
rökt renstek rurkt reen·steek	smoked reindeer
rökt skinka rurkt shihng·ka	smoked ham
sadel sah·dehl	saddle (cut of meat)
salamikorv sa·lah·mee·kohrv	salami
schnitzel shniht·sehl	escallope

With/Without…	**Med/Utan…** meed/eu·tan…
I can't have…	**Jag kan inte äta mat som innehåller…** yahg kan ihn·ter air·ta maht som ih·neh·hoal·lehr…

sjömansbiff shur·mans·bihf	casserole of fried beef, onions and potatoes, braised in beer
skinka shihng·ka	ham
spädgris spaird·grees	an unweaned piglet
stekt kyckling steekt chewk·lihng	fried chicken (not breaded)
T-benstek tee·been·steek	T-bone steak
tunga tuhng·a	tongue (cow)
ugnsstekt kyckling eungn·steekt chewk·lihng	roast chicken
vaktel vak·tehl	quail
varmkorv varm·kohrv	hot dog
wienerschnitzel vee·nehr·shniht·sehl	breaded veal cutlet
vildand vihld·and	wild duck
vilt vihlt	game
älg ehly	moose
älgfilé ehly·fih·leh	fillet of moose
älgstek ehly·steek	moose roast
älgstek med svampsås ehly·steek meed svamp·soas	roast moose with mushroom sauce

rare	**blodig** bloa·dihg
medium	**medium** mee·dee·uhm
well done	**genomstekt** ye·nom·steekt

I'd like…	**Jag skulle vilja ha…** yahg skuh·ler vihl·ya hah…
More…, please.	**Lite mer…, tack.** lee·teh meer…tak

Swedish Buffet: Smorgasbord

blandsallad bland•sal•ad	mixed salad
efterrätt ehf•tehr•reht	dessert
grönsak grurn•sahk	vegetable
grönsallad grurn•sal•ad	green salad
Janssons frestelse yahn•sons frehs•tehl•ser	casserole with potatoes and anchovies
korv kohrv	sausage
köttbulle churt•buh•ler	meatball
omelett ohm•eh•leht	omelet
ostbricka oast•brih•ka	cheese plate
potatissallad poa•tah•tihs•sal•ad	potato salad
sillsallad sihl•sal•ad	beet and herring salad
skaldjurssallad skahl•yeurs•sal•ad	shellfish salad
skarpsill skarp•sihl	herring
tomater och lök toa•mah•ter ohk lurk	tomato and onion salad
västkustsallad vehst•kuhst•sal•ad	west coast salad, with shrimp [prawns] and mussels

With/Without...	**Med/Utan...** meed/eu•tan...
I can't have...	**Jag kan inte äta mat som innehåller...** yahg kan ihn•ter air•ta maht som ih•neh•hoal•lehr...

If you've never heard of typical Swedish food, you may at at least be familiar with the famous **smörgåsbord**—it is a buffet meal on a grand scale, presented on a large, beautifully decorated table. You start at one end of the table, usually the one with the cold seafood dishes, marinated herring, **Janssons frestelse** (literally, Jansson's temptation, a potato and anchovies casserole) and salad. Then you work your way through the cold meat, meatballs, sausage, omelets and vegetables. Finally, you end at the cheeseboard and desserts. You're welcome to start all over again; the price is set, and you can eat as much as you like. You will find that the Swedes tend to drink **akvavit** (aquavit) or beer with the feast, although an accompanying glass of wine is becoming more common for those who find **akvavit** too strong.

At Christmas time, the **smörgåsbord** becomes a **julbord** (Christmas buffet), served in homes and restaurants alike.

Vegetables

avokado a•voh•kah•doa	avocado
blomkål bloam•koal	cauliflower
böna… bur•na…	…bean
– **bond** boand	– broad
– **bryt** brewt	– kidney
– **grön** grurn	– green
– **vax** vax	– butter
broccoli broh•koh•lee	broccoli
brysselkål brew•sehl•koal	Brussel sprout
bönskott burn•skoht	bean sprout

I'd like…	**Jag skulle vilja ha…** yahg skuh•ler vihl•ya hah…
More…, please.	**Lite mer…, tack.** lee•teh meer…tak

champinjon sham•pihn•<u>yoan</u>	mushroom
endiv an•<u>deev</u>	endive
färskpotatis <u>fairsk</u>•poa•<u>tah</u>•tihs	new potato
gräslök <u>grairs</u>•lurk	chive
grön paprika grurn <u>pah</u>•pree•ka	green pepper
grönsak <u>grurn</u>•sahk	vegetable
grönsallad <u>grurn</u>•sal•ad	lettuce
gurka <u>geur</u>•ka	cucumber
haricots verts ar•ee•koh•<u>vair</u>	green bean
kantarell kan•ta•<u>rehl</u>	chanterelle mushroom
kikärta <u>cheek</u>•air•ta	chickpea
kokt potatis koakt poa•<u>tah</u>•tihs	boiled potato
kronärtskocka <u>kroan</u>•airts•koh•ka	artichoke
kål koal	cabbage
kålrot <u>koal</u>•roht	turnip

With/Without...	**Med/Utan...** meed/<u>eu</u>•tan...
I can't have...	**Jag kan inte äta mat som innehåller...** yahg kan <u>ihn</u>•ter <u>air</u>•ta maht som <u>ih</u>•neh•hoal•lehr...

källkrasse chehl·kra·ser — watercress
lins lihns — lentil
lök lurk — onion
majs mays — sweet corn
morot moa·roht — carrot
palsternacka pal·stehr·na·ka — parsnip
paprika pah·prih·ka — pepper (fresh)
potatis poa·tah·tihs — potato
pumpa puhm·pa — pumpkin
purjolök peur·yoh·lurk — leek
rova roa·va — turnip
rädisa raid·dih·sa — radish
röd paprika rurd pah·pree·ka — sweet red pepper
rödbeta rurd·bee·ta — beet
rödkål rurd·koal — red cabbage
salladshuvud sal·ads·heu·vuhd — head of lettuce
saltgurka salt·geur·ka — salted, pickled gherkin
schalottenlök sha·loh·tehn·lurk — shallot [spring onion]
selleri seh·leh·ree — celery
skogssvamp skoags·svamp — field mushroom
sockerärta soh·kehr·air·ta — sugar snap pea [mangetout]
sparris spar·ihs — asparagus
spenat speh·naht — spinach
squash skoawsh — squash (vegetable)

I'd like…	**Jag skulle vilja ha…** yahg skuh·ler vihl·ya hah…
More…, please.	**Lite mer…, tack.** lee·teh meer…tak

svamp svamp	mushroom
sötpotatis surt·poa·tah·tihs	sweet potato
tomat toa·maht	tomato
vattenkrasse kra·ser	watercress
vild champinjon vihl·da sham·pihn·yoan	wild mushroom
vitkål veet·koal	white cabbage
vitlök veet·lurk	garlic
vårlök voar·lurk	shallot [spring onion]
zucchini seu·kee·nee	zucchini [courgette]
äggplanta ehg·plan·ta	eggplant [aubergine]
ärta air·ta	peas
ättiksgurka eh·tiks·geur·kah	pickled gherkin

Spices and Staples

basilika ba·sih·lee·ka	basil
bouquet garni boh·keh gar·nee	mixed herbs
bröd brurd	bread
chilipeppar shee·lih·peh·par	chili pepper
dragon dra·goan	tarragon
fänkål fehn·koal	fennel
fullkornsmjöl fuhl·kohrns·myurl	whole wheat flour
honung hoa·neung	honey
ingefära ih·ng·eh·fai·ra	ginger

With/Without...	**Med/Utan...** meed/eu·tan...
I can't have...	**Jag kan inte äta mat som innehåller...** yahg kan ihn·ter air·ta maht som ih·neh·hoal·lehr...

kanel ka·neel	cinnamon
kapris ka·prees	caper
kryddpeppar krewd·peh·par	allspice
kummin keu·meen	caraway
körvel chur·vehl	chervil
lagerblad lah·gehr·blahd	bay leaf
mjöl myurl	flour
muskot muhs·koht	nutmeg
mynta mewn·ta	mint (herb)
nejlika nay·lih·ka	clove
nudel neu·dehl	noodle
olja och vinäger oal·ya ohk vee·nai·gehr	oil and vinegar
pasta pas·ta	pasta
peppar peh·par	pepper
persilja pair·shihl·ya	parsley
ris rees	rice
rosmarin roas·ma·reen	rosemary
salt salt	salt
salvia sal·vee·a	sage
senap see·nap	mustard
sirap seh·rap	syrup
socker soh·kehr	sugar
smör smurr	butter

I'd like…	**Jag skulle vilja ha…** yahg skuh·ler vihl·ya hah…
More…, please.	**Lite mer…, tack.** lee·teh meer…tak

sötningsmedel surt·nihngs·mee·dehl | artificial sweetener
timjan tihm·yan | thyme
vanilj va·nihly | vanilla
vetemjöl vee·teh·mjurl | wheat flour (regular)

Fruit and Nuts

ananas an·a·nas | pineapple
apelsin a·pehl·seen | orange
aprikos a·prih·koas | apricot
banan ba·nahn | banana
bigarrå bih·ga·roa | sweet morello cherry
björnbär byurn·bair | blackberry
blå vindruva bloa veen·dreu·va | black grape
blåbär bloa·bair | blueberry
citron see·troan | lemon
dadel dahd·ehl | date
enbär een·bair | juniper berry
fikon fee·kohn | fig
frukt fruhkt | fruit
grapefrukt grape·fruhkt | grapefruit
grön vindruva grurn veen·dreu·va | green grape
hallon hal·ohn | raspberry
hasselnöt ha·sehl·nurt | hazelnut
hjortron yoahr·tron | cloudberry

With/Without…	**Med/Utan…** meed/eu·tan…
I can't have…	**Jag kan inte äta mat som innehåller…** yahg kan ihn·ter air·ta maht som ih·neh·hoal·lehr…

jordgubbe yoard·guh·ber	strawberry
jordnöt yoard·nurt	peanut
katrinplommon ka·treen·ploa·mohn	prune
kiwifrukt kee·vee·fruhkt	kiwi
kokosnöt koa·kos·nurt	coconut
krusbär kreus·bair	gooseberry
körsbär churs·bair	cherry
lingon lihng·ohn	lingonberry
mandarin man·da·reen	tangerine/mandarin orange
mandel man·dehl	almond
(vatten)melon (va·tehrn)meh·loan	(water)melon
mullbär muhl·bair	mulberry
nektarin nehk·ta·reen	nectarine
oliv o·leev	olive
persika pairsh·ih·ka	peach
plommon plohm·on	plum
pomegranat äpple pom·eh·gra·naht·ehp·leh	pomegranate
päron pai·rohn	pear
rabarber rah·bar·behr	rhubarb
russin ruh·sihn	raisin
röd vinbär rurd veen·bair	red currant
smultron smeul·trohn	wild strawberry
sultana suhl·tahn·a	sultana raisin
svart vinbär svart veen·bair	black currant

I'd like…	**Jag skulle vilja ha…** yahg skuh·ler vihl·ya hah…
More…, please.	**Lite mer…, tack.** lee·teh meer…tak

valnöt vahl·nurt	walnut
vinbär veen·bair	currant
vindruva veen·dreu·va	grape
äpple ehp·leh	apple

Cheese

fårost foar·oast	ewe's milk cheese
getost yeet·oast	goat cheese
grevé greh·vee	a semi-hard cheese with a taste between gouda and emmentaler
herrgårdsost hehr·goards·oast	a semi-hard cheese with large holes and a nutty flavor
kryddost krewd·oast	a sharp, strong cheese with caraway seeds
mesost mees·oast	a soft, sweet, yellowish whey cheese
mjukost myeuk·oast	soft cheese
ost oast	cheese
prästost prehst·oast	hard cheese with a strong, rich flavor
svecia sveh·see·a	semi-hard cheeses
västerbotten vehs·tehr·boh·tehrn	a sharp, tangy, hard and very strong cheese from the north of Sweden

With/Without…	**Med/Utan…** meed/eu·tan…
I can't have…	**Jag kan inte äta mat som innehåller…** yahg kan ihn·ter air·ta maht som ih·neh·hoal·lehr…

ädelost air·dehl·oast	a blue cheese with a sharp taste, similar to roquefort

Dessert

efterrätt ehf·tehr·reht	dessert
friterad camembert med hjortronsylt free·tee·rad cam·ehm·behrt meed yoh·tron·sewlt	deep-fried camembert with cloudberry jam
fruktsallad fruhkt·sal·ad	fruit salad
glass glas	ice cream
jordgubbar med grädde yoard·guhb·ar meed greh·deh	strawberries and cream
kaka kah·ka	cake
mandeltårta man·dehl·toar·ta	almond tart
marängsviss mah·rehng·svis	meringue with whipped cream and chocolate sauce
mjuk pepparkaka myeuk peh·par·kah·ka	soft ginger cake
ostkaka oast·kah·ka	traditional southern Sweden curd cake
tårta toarta	sponge-based fruit or cream cake
våffla (med sylt och grädde) vohf·la meed sewlt ohk greh·der	waffle (with jam and whipped cream)
äppelpaj eh·pehl·pay	apple tart
äppelkaka eh·pehl·kah·ka	apple cake
äppelring ehp·ehl·rihng	apple fritter

I'd like…	**Jag skulle vilja ha…** yahg skuh·ler vihl·ya hah…
More…, please.	**Lite mer…, tack.** lee·teh meer…tak

Drinks

Essential

May I see the *wine list/drink menu*?	**Kan jag få se *vinlistan/drinklistan*?** kan yahg f**oa** see *veen·lihs·tan/drihnk·lihs·tan*
What do you recommend?	**Vad rekommenderar ni?** vahd reh·koh·mehn·**dee**·rar nee
I'd like a *bottle/glass* of *red/white* wine.	**Jag skulle vilja ha *en flaska/ett glas rött/vitt* vin.** yahg skuh·ler vihl·ya hah *ehn flas·ka/eht glahs ruhrt/viht* veen
The house wine, please.	**Husets vin, tack.** heu·sehts veen tak
Another *bottle/glass*, please.	***En flaska/Ett glas* till, tack.** *ehn flas·ka/eht glahs* tihl tak
I'd like a local beer.	**Jag skulle vilja ha en öl från trakten.** yahg skuh·ler vihl·ya hah ehn **ur**l fron trak·tehn
Let me buy you a drink.	**Får jag bjuda på en drink.** fo**a**r yahg by**eu**·da p**oa** ehn drihnk
Cheers!	**Skål!** sko**a**l
A *coffee/tea*, please.	**En kopp *kaffe/te*, tack.** ehn kohp *ka·fer/tee* tak
Black.	**Svart.** svart
With...	**Med...** meed...
– milk	**– mjölk** myuhlk
– sugar	**– socker** soh·kehr
– artificial sweetener	**– sötningsmedel** surt·nihngs·mee·dehl
– decaf	**– utan koffein** eu·tan koh·feen
..., please.	**..., tack.** ...tak
– Juice	**– Juice** yoas
– Soda	**– sodavatten** soa·da·va·tehrn

– (*Sparkling/Still*) Water	**– Vatten (*med/utan* kolsyra)** va•tehrn (*meed/eu•tan* koal•s**ew**•ra)
Is the tap water safe to drink?	**Kan man dricka kranvattnet?** kan man drih•ka krahn•vat•neht

Non-alcoholic Drinks

alkoholfri dryck al•ko•h**oa**l•free drewk — non-alcoholic drink

ananasjuice an•a•nas•yoas — pineapple juice

apelsinjuice a•pehl•seen•yoas — orange juice

cola koa•la — cola

fruktjuice fruhkt•yoas — fruit juice

juice yoas — juice

kaffe ka•fer — coffee

läsk lehsk — soft drink

milkshake milk•shake — milk shake

mineralvatten mihn•eh•rahl•va•tehrn — mineral water

mjölk my**ur**lk — milk

saft saft — squash (fruit cordial)

sockerdricka soh•kehr•drih•ka — lemonade

sodavatten soa•da•va•tehrn — soda water

thé med *mjölk/citron* tee meed *myurlk/see•troan* — tea with *milk/lemon*

tomatjuice toa•maht•yoas — tomato juice

tonic toh•nihk — tonic water

varmchoklad varm shoa•klahd — hot chocolate

vatten *med/utan* kolsyra va•tehrn *meed/eu•tan* koal•s**ew**•ra — *sparkling/still* water

i For afternoon tea (usually enjoyed with lemon) or coffee you can do no better than the typical Swedish **konditori** (patisserie or coffee shop). Help yourself to as many cups as you like while indulging in a slice of **prinsesstårta** (sponge cake with cream and custard, covered with green marzipan), **mazarin** (almond tart, topped with icing) or a **wienerbröd** (Danish pastry). Try **saffransbullar** (saffron buns) and **pepparkakor** (ginger cookies) at Christmas. Most **konditori** are self-service, but some of the more elegant ones and those in hotels provide full service. Coffee is definitely the national drink, and it is always freshly brewed. It is commonly drunk black, but ask for **mjölk** (milk) or **grädde** (cream) if you like it that way.

You May Hear...

Får jag bjuda på en drink? foar yahg <u>bjeu</u>•da pao ehn drink	Can I buy you a drink?
Med *mjölk/socker*? meed *myurlk/<u>soh</u>•ker*	With *milk/sugar*?
Vatten *med/utan* kolsyra? <u>va</u>•tehrn *meed/ <u>eu</u>•tan* <u>koal</u>•sew•ra	*Sparkling/Still* water?

Aperitifs, Cocktails and Liqueurs

akvavit a·kva·veet	aquavit, the famous Swedish grain- or potato-based spirit
cognac kohn·yak	brandy
gin jihn	gin
glögg glurg	mulled wine with port and spices, served hot
herrgårdsakvavit hair·goards·a·kva·veet	aquavit, flavored with caraway seeds and whisky
likör lih·kurr	liqueur
portvin port·veen	port
punsch peunsh	sweet liqueur
rom rohm	rum
sherry sheh·ree	sherry
skåne skoa·ner	aquavit, flavored with aniseed and caraway seeds
sprit spreet	spirits
vermouth vehr·meutt	vermouth
vodka… vod·ka…	vodka…
– med is meed ees	– on the rocks [with ice]
– med tonic meed toh·nihk	– with tonic water
– med vatten meed va·tehrn	– with water
whisky vihs·kee	whisky

Beer

burköl buhrk·**url**	canned beer
fatöl faht·**url**	draft [draught]
lättöl leht·**url**	light beer
öl på flaska **url** poa fla·ska	bottled beer

Beer is probably the most popular alcoholic drink in Sweden, and there are many good Swedish breweries. Beer with an alcohol content above 3%, called **starköl**, can only be bought in **Systembolaget** (state liquor store); **lättöl** and **folköl**, which are below 3% alcohol content, can be bought in grocery stores and supermarkets. You will find many well known international beers, but the most common are Carlsberg, Heineken and Swedish brews such as Pripps and Falcon.

Wine

dessertvin deh·sair·veen	dessert wine
husets vin heu·sehts veen	house wine
mousserande moa·see·ran·der	sparkling
rosé roh·seh	blush [rosé]
rött ruhrt	red
sött suhrt	sweet
torrt tohrt	dry
vitt viht	white

Menu Reader

abborre ah·bohr·er — perch

akvavit a·kva·veet — aquavit, the famous Swedish grain- or potato-based spirit

alkoholfri dryck al·ko·hoal·free drewk — non-alcoholic drink

ananas an·a·nas — pineapple

ananasjuice an·a·nas·yoas — pineapple juice

anka ang·ka — duck

ansjovis an·shoa·vees — anchovy

apelsin a·pehl·seen — orange

apelsinjuice a·pehl·seen·yoas — orange juice

aprikos a·prih·koas — apricot
avokado a·voh·kah·doa — avocado
bacon bay·kon — bacon
bakelse bah·kehl·sehr — piece of cake
bakverk bahk·verk — pastry
banan ba·nahn — banana
basilika ba·sih·lee·ka — basil
biffkött bihf·churt — beef
biffstek bif·steek — steak
bigarrå bih·ga·roa — sweet morello cherry
bit beet — slice
björnbär byurn·bair — blackberry
blandade blan·da·der — assorted
blandade grönsaker blan·da·der grurn·sah·kehr — mixed vegetables
blandade kryddor blan·da·der krew·dohr — mixed herbs
blandade nötter blan·da·der nur·tehr — assorted nuts
blandsallad bland·sal·ad — mixed salad
blodig bloa·dihg — rare
blomkål bloam·koal — cauliflower
blå vindruva bloa veen·dreu·va — black grape
blåbär bloa·bair — blueberry
blåbärssylt bloa·bairs·sewlt — blueberry jam
blåmussla bloa·muhs·la — blue mussel
bog boag — shoulder (cut of meat)
bondböna boand·bur·nohr — broad bean
bordsvin boards·veen — table wine
bouquet garni boh·keh gar·nee — mixed herbs

braxen brak·sehn	sea bream
broccoli broh·loh·lee	broccoli
broiler broy·lehr	spring chicken
brylépudding brew·lee·peu·dihng	crème brulee
brysselkål brew·sehl·koal	brussel sprout
brytböna brewt·bur·na	kidney bean
brännvin brehn·veen	aquavit, grain or potato based spirit
bröd brurd	bread
brödsmulor brurd·smeu·lohr	bread crumbs
bröst brurst	breast
buljong buhl·yong	broth
bulle buh·ler	bun
burköl buhrk·url	canned beer
bål boal	punch
böckling burk·lihng	smoked herring
böna bur·na	bean [pulses]
bönskott burn·skoht	bean sprout
champinjon sham·pihn·yoan	mushroom
chilipeppar shee·lih·peh·par	chili pepper
chips shihps	potato chips [crisps]
choklad shoa·klahd	chocolate
citron see·troan	lemon
citronjuice see·troan·yoas	lemon juice
cognac kohn·yak	brandy
cola koa·la	cola
dadel dahd·ehl	date
dagens meny dah·gehns meh·neu	menu of the day

dagens rätt dah·gehns rairtt — speciality of the day
dessertvin deh·sair·veen — dessert wine
dillsås dihl·soas — dill sauce
dragon dra·goan — tarragon
dryck med alkohol drewk meed al·ko·hoal — alcoholic drink
efterrätt ehf·tehr·rairt — dessert
en halv flaska ehn halv fla·ska — half bottle
enbär een·bair — juniper berry
endiv an·deev — endive
entrecote an·treh·koa — sirloin steak
falukorv fah·leu·kohrv — lightly spiced sausage
fasan fa·sahn — pheasant
fatöl faht·url — draft [draught] beer
fikon fee·kohn — fig
filé fih·leh — filet mignon
filmjölk feel·mjurlk — thick yogurt
fisk fihsk — fish
fisk och skaldjur fihsk·ohk·skahl·yeur — fish and seafood
fisksoppa fihsk·sop·a — fish soup
fläsk flehsk — pork
fläskben flehsk·been — ham bone
fläskfilé flehsk·fih·leh — fillet of pork
fläskkarré flehsk·ka·reh — pork loin
fläskkorv flehsk·kohrv — spicy, boiled pork sausage
fläsklägg flehsk·lehg — knuckle of pork
fläskpannkaka flehsk·pan·kah·ka — thick pancake filled with bacon

forell foa·rehl	trout
franskbröd fransk·brurd	French bread
friterad camembert med hjortronsylt free·tee·rad cam·ehm·behrt meed yoh·tron·sewlt	deep-fried Camembert with cloudberry jam
frukost fruh·kohst	breakfast
frukostflingor fruhkost·flihng·ohr	(cold) cereal
frukt fruhkt	fruit
fruktjuice fruhkt·yoas	fruit juice
fruktsallad fruhkt·sal·ad	fruit salad
fullkornsmjöl fuhl·kohrns·myurl	whole wheat flour
fylld (med) fewld (meed)	stuffed (with)
fylld oliv fewld o·leev	stuffed olive
fylligt few·liht	full-bodied (wine)
fågel foa·gehl	poultry
får foar	mutton
fårost foar·oast	ewe's milk cheese
fänkål fehn·koal	fennel
färsk (frukt) fehrsk (fruhkt)	fresh (fruit)
färsk fikon fairsk fee·kohn	fresh fig
färska räkor fairs·ka rair·kohr	unshelled shrimp [prawns]
färskpotatis fairsk·poa·tah·tihs	new potato
förlorat ägg furr·loa·rat ehg	poached egg
förrätt furr·rairt	appetizer [starter]
garnering gar·nee·rihng	garnish
gelé sheh·leh	jelly
get yeet	kid (goat)
getost yeet·oast	goat cheese

gin jihn — gin

glass glas — ice cream

glutenfritt glue·tehn·friht — gluten free

glögg glurg — mulled wine with port and spices, served hot

grapefrukt grahp·fruhkt — grapefruit

gratinerad gra·tih·nee·rad — au gratin

gratäng gra·tehng — casserole

gravlax grafv·lax — marinated salmon

grevé greh·veh — semi-hard cheese

grillad kyckling grihl·ahd chewk·lihng — grilled chicken

grillspett grihl·speht — skewer

gryta grew·ta — pot roast, stew or casserole

grädde greh·der — cream

gräddfil grehd·feel — sour cream

gräslök grairs·lurk — chive

grön böna grur·na bur·na — green bean

grön paprika grurn pah·pree·ka — green pepper

grön vindruva grurn veen·dreu·va — green grape

grönsak grurn·sahk — vegetable

grönsakssoppa grurn·sahks·sohp·a — vegetable soup

grönsallad grurn·sal·ad — green salad

gröt grurt — (hot) cereal

gurka geur·ka — cucumber

gås goas — goose

gädda yeh·da — sea perch

hallon hal·ohn — raspberry

halstrad fisk hal·strahd fihsk	grilled fish
halstrad forell med färskpotatis hal·strad foa·rehl med fairsk·poa·tah·tihs	grilled trout with new potatoes
hamburgare ham·beur·ya·rer	hamburger
hare hah·rer	rabbit
haricots verts ar·ee·koh·vair	string beans
hasselbackspotatis ha·sehl·baks·poa·tah·tihs	oven-baked potato, coated in bread crumbs
hasselnöt ha·sehl·nurt	hazelnut
havre hafv·rer	oats
havregryn hafv·reh·greun	oatmeal
havsabborre hafs·a·boh·rer	sea bass
hemlagad hehm·lah·gad	homemade
herrgårdsakvavit hair·goards·a·kva·veet	aquavit flavored with caraway seeds and whisky
herrgårdsost hehr·goards·oast	semi-hard cheese with a nutty flavor
hett heht	hot (temperature)
hjort yohrt	deer
hjortron yoahr·tron	cloudberry
hjortron sylt yoar·trohn·sewlt	cloudberry jam
honung hoa·neung	honey
hovmästarsås hoav·mehs·tar·soas	dill sauce
hummer huhm·ehr	lobster
husets specialitet heu·sehts speh·sih·al·ee·teet	specialty of the house
husets vin heu·sehts veen	house wine
huvudrätt heu·vuhd·rait	main course

hårdkokt ägg hoard·kohkt ehg	hard-boiled egg
hårt bröd hoart brurd	crispbread
hälleflundra heh·leh·fleun·dra	halibut
ingefära ih·ng·eh·fai·ra	ginger
inlagd i ättika (vinäger) ihn·lahgd ee eh·tih·ka	marinated in vinegar
inlagd sill ihn·lahgd sil	marinated (pickled) herring
is ees	ice
isterband ihs·tehr·band	sausage of pork, barley and beef
Janssons frestelse yahn·sons frehs·tehl·ser	casserole with potatoes and anchovies
jordgubbar med grädde yoard·guhb·ar meed greh·deh	strawberries and cream
jordgubbe yoard·guh·ber	strawberry
jordnöt yoard·nurt	peanut
juice yoas	juice
julbord yeul·board	buffet of hot and cold Swedish specialties served at Christmas time
kaffe ka·fer	coffee
kaka kah·ka	cake
kalkon kal·koan	turkey
kall soppa kal sohp·a	cold soup
kallskuret kal·skeu·reht	cold cuts
kalops ka·lohps	beef stew
kalvbräss kalv·brehs	sweetbread

kalvkött kalv·churt	veal
kalvsylta kalv·sewl·ta	cold veal in jelly
kammussla kam·muhs·la	scallop
kanderad frukt kan·deeh·rahd fruhkt	candied fruit
kanel ka·neel	cinnamon
kantarell kan·ta·rehl	chanterelle mushroom
kapris ka·prees	caper
karaff ka·raff	carafe
karameller ka·ra·mehl·ehr	candy [sweets]
karré ka·reh	tenderloin
katrinplommon ka·treen·ploa·mohn	prune
kex kehx	cookie [biscuit]
kikärta cheek·air·ta	chickpea
kiwifrukt kee·vee·fruhkt	kiwi
klimp klihmp	dumpling
kokosnöt koa·kos·nurt	coconut
kokt katrinplommon koakt ka·treen·ploa·mohn	stewed prune
kokt potatis koakt poa·tah·tihs	boiled potato
kokt skinka koakt shihng·ka	boiled ham
kokt ägg koakt ehg	boiled egg
kolja kohl·ya	haddock
kolsyrad koal·sew·rad	carbonated
kompott kom·poht	stewed fruit
konserverad frukt kon·ser·vee·rad fruhkt	canned fruit
korv kohrv	sausage
kotlett koht·lehtt	cutlet
krabba kra·ba	crab

kronärtskocka kroan·airts·koh·ka — artichoke

kroppkaka kropp·kah·ka — potato dumpling, filled with bacon and onions

krusbär kreus·bair — gooseberry

krydda krew·da — spice

kryddad krew·dad — spicy

kryddad pepparsås krew·dahd peh·par·soas — hot pepper sauce

kryddost krewd·oast — sharp, strong cheese with caraway seeds

kryddpeppar krewd·peh·par — allspice

kryddstarkt krewd·starkt — spicy

kräfta krehf·ta — crayfish

kummel keu·mel — hake

kummin keu·meen — caraway

kvark kvark — fresh curd cheese

kyckling chewk·lihng — chicken

kycklingbröst chewk·lihng·brurst — chicken breast

kycklinglever chewk·lihng·lee·vehr — chicken liver

kycklingsoppa chewk·lihng·sohp·a — chicken soup

kyld dryck chewl drewk — cold drink

kylt chewlt — chilled (wine, etc.)

kål koal — cabbage

kåldolmar koal·dohl·mar — cabbage leaves stuffed with chopped [minced] meat and rice

kålrot koal·roht — turnip

källkrasse chehl·kra·se — watercress

körsbär churs·bair — cherry

körvel chur·vehl	chervil
kött churt	meat
kött och grönsakssoppa churt·oa·grurn·sahk·sohp·a	meat and vegetable soup
köttbulle churt·buh·ler	meatball
köttfärs churt·fairs	chopped [minced] beef
köttsoppa churt·sohp·a	beef and vegetable soup with dumplings
köttsås churt·soas	meat sauce
lagerblad lah·gehr·blahd	bay leaf
lageröl lah·ger·url	lager
lamm lamm	lamb
lammgryta lamm·grew·ta	lamb stew
landgång land·goang	long open-faced sandwich
lax lax	salmon
lever lee·vehr	liver
leverpastej lee·vehr pa·stay	liver pâté
lingon lihng·ohn	lingonberry
lingonsylt lihng·ohn·sewlt	lingonberry jam
lins lihns	lentil
likör lih·kurr	liqueur
lägg lehg	shank (top of leg)
läsk lehsk	soft drink
lättöl leht·ur	light beer
löjrom lury·rohm	bleak roe with chopped, raw onions and sour cream; served on toast

lök lurk — onion

löksoppa lurk·sohp·a — onion soup

lövbiff lurv·bihf — fried, thinly sliced beef, with onions

majonnäs may·oha·nairs — mayonnaise

majs mays — sweet corn

makrill mahk·rihl — mackerel

mandarin man·da·reen — tangerine/mandarin orange

mandel man·dehl — almond

mandeltårta man·dehl·toar·ta — almond tart

marmelad mahr·meh·lahd — marmalade

marsipan mahr·sih·pahn — marzipan

marulk mahr·eulk — monkfish

maräng mah·rehng — meringue

marängsviss mah·rehng·svihs — meringue served with cream and chocolate sauce

matjesill ma·shcheh·sihl — marinated herring

med citron meed see·troan — with lemon

med florsocker meed floar·soh·ker — with icing

med grädde meed greh·der — with cream

med is meed ees — with ice

med kolsyra meed koal·sew·ra — carbonated (drink)

med mjölk meed myurlk — with milk

med socker meed soh·kehr — with sugar

med tonic meed toh·nihk — with tonic water

med vatten meed va·tehrn — with water

med vitlök meed veet·lurk — with garlic

medaljong meh·dal·yong	small fillet of cut meat
medium meh·dee·yuhm	medium
mellanmål meh·lan·moal	snack
(vatten)melon (va·tehrn)meh·loan	(water)melon
meny meh·neu	menu
mesost mees·oast	soft, sweet whey cheese
middag mih·dahg	dinner
milkshake milk·shake	milk shake
mineralvatten mih·neh·rahl·va·tehrn	mineral water
mjuk pepparkaka myeuk peh·par·kah·ka	soft ginger cake
mjukost myeuk·oast	soft cheese
mjöl myurl	flour
mjölk myurlk	milk
mogen moa·gehn	ripe
morot moa·roht	carrot
mousserande moa·see·ran·der	sparkling (wine)
muffin muh·fihn	muffin
mullbär muhl·bair	mulberry
multe muhl·ter	mullet
munk muhnk	donut
muskot muhs·koht	nutmeg
müsli mews·lee	granola [muesli]
mussla muhs·la	mussel
mustigt muhs·tihkt	full-bodied (wine)
mycket kryddad mew·keht krew·dad	highly seasoned
mycket torrt mew·keht tohrt	very dry (wine, etc.)
mynta mewn·ta	mint (herb)

mäktig	mehk·tihg	rich (sauce)
mördegstårta	muhr·deegs·**toar**·ta	tart (sweet or savory)
mört	murtt	roach (type of fish)
nejlika	nay·lih·ka	clove
nektarin	nehk·ta·reen	nectarine
njure	nyeu·rer	kidney
nudel	neu·dehl	noodle
nyponsoppa	new·pohn·sohp·a	rose-hip soup
nötkött	nurt·churt	red meat
odlade champinjon	oad·lah·der sham·peen·**yoa**n	cultivated mushroom
ojäst bröd	oa·**yair**st br**ur**d	unleavened bread
oliv	o·leev	olive
olja och vinäger	oal·ya ohk vee·**nai**·gehr	oil and vinegar
omelett	om·eh·leht	omelet
ost	oast	cheese
ostbricka	oast·brih·ka	cheese plate
ostkaka	oast·kah·ka	curd cake served with jam
ostkex	oast·kehx	cheese cracker
ostron	oa·strohn	oyster
oxkött	oax·churt	ox
oxrullad	oax·reu·lahd	braised roll of beef
oxsvans	oax·svans	oxtail
oxsvanssoppa	oax·svans·sohp·a	oxtail soup
paj	pay	pie
palsternacka	pal·stehr·na·ka	parsnip
pannbiff	pan·bihf	beef patty

pannkaka pan·kah·ka — pancake
paprika pah·prih·ka — pepper (fresh)
pasta pas·ta — pasta
pastarätt pas·ta·rairt — pasta dish
pastej pa·stay — pâté
peppar peh·par — pepper (condiment)
pepparkaka peh·par·kah·ka — ginger cookie
pepparrotssås peh·pa·roat·soas — horseradish sauce
persika pair·shih·ka — peach
persilja pair·shihl·ya — parsley
piggvar pihg·vahr — turbot
pitabröd pee·ta·brurd — pita bread
plommon ploa·mohn — plum
plättar pleh·tar — small pancakes served with jam and whipped cream
pomegranat äpple pom·eh·gra·naht·ehp·leh — pomegranate
pommes frites pohm·friht — French fries
portion pohrt·shoan — portion
portvin pohrt·veen — port
potatis poa·tah·tihs — potato
potatismos poa·tah·tihs·moas — mashed potatoes
potatissoppa poa·tah·tihs·sohp·a — potato soup
prinsesstårta prihn·sehs·toar·ta — sponge cake with (vanilla) custard, whipped cream and jam, covered in light green marzipan
prinskorv prihns·kohrv — small pork sausage

prästost prehst·oast hard cheese with a strong, rich flavor

pumpa puhm·pa pumpkin

punsch peunsh sweet liqueur

purjolök peur·yoh·lurk leek

pytt i panna pewt·ee·pa·na chunks of fried meat, onion and potatoes

på beställning poa beh·stehl·nihng made on request

pärlande pair·lan·der sparkling

pärlhöns pairl·hurns guinea fowl

päron pai·rohn pear

rabarber rah·bar·behr rhubarb

ragu ra·gue beef stew

rapphöna rap·hurna partridge

ren reen reindeer

renat ree·nat flavorless, clear spirit (aquavit)

renstek reen·steek roast reindeer

revbensspjäll reev·beens·spehl spareribs

riktigt blodig rihk·tihgt bloa·dihg very rare

rimmad lax rih·mad lax lightly salted salmon

ris rees rice

rocka roh·ka ray (type of fish)

rom rohm rum

rosé roh·seh blush (wine)

rosmarin roas·ma·reen rosemary

rostat bröd rohs·tat brurd toast

rostbiff rohst·bihf roast beef

rova roa·va turnip

rumpstek ruhmp·steek	rump steak
russin ruh·sihn	raisin
rå roa	raw
rådjur roa·yeur	venison
rådjursstek roa·yeur·steek	roast of venison
rågbröd roag·brurd	rye bread
rädisa raid·dih·sa	radish
räkor rair·kohr	shrimp [prawns]
rätt reht	dish
röd paprika rurd pah·pree·ka	sweet red pepper
röd vinbär rurd veen·bair	red currant
rödbeta rurd·bee·ta	beet
röding rur·dihng	char
rödkål rurd·koal	red cabbage
rödspätta rurd·speh·ta	plaice
rökt fisk rurkt fisk	smoked fish
rökt lax rurkt lax	smoked salmon
rökt renstek rurkt reen·steek	smoked reindeer
rökt skinka rurkt shihng·ka	smoked ham
rökt ål rurkt oal	smoked eel
rörd soppa rurrd sohp·a	cream soup
rött rurt	red (wine)
sadel sah·dehl	saddle (cut of meat)
saffransbullar sa·frans·buh·lar	Christmas saffron buns
saft saft	squash (fruit cordial)
salamikorv sa·lah·mee·kohrv	salami
sallad sal·ad	salad

salladshuvud sal·ads·heu·vuhd	head of lettuce
salt salt	salt
saltade jordnötter sal·ta·der yoard·nur·ter	salted peanuts
saltgurka salt·geur·ka	salted, pickled gherkin
salvia sal·vee·a	sage
sardin sar·deen	sardine
schalottenlök sha·loh·tehn·lurk	shallot
schnitzel shniht·sehl	escallope
selleri seh·leh·ree	celery
senap see·nap	mustard
sherry sheh·ree	sherry
sill sihl	herring
sillbricka sihl·brih·ka	variety of marinated herring
sillsallad sihl·sal·ad	beet and herring salad
sirap seh·rap	syrup
sjömansbiff shur·mans·bihf	casserole of fried beef, onions and potatoes, braised in beer
sjötunga sjur·teung·a	sole
skaldjur skahl·yeur	shellfish
skaldjurssallad skahl·yeurs·sal·ad	shellfish salad
skarpsill skarp·sihl	herring
skinka skihng·ka	ham
skogssvamp skoags·svamp	field mushroom
sky shewy	gravy
skåne skoa·ner	type of aquavit flavored with aniseed and caraway

smultron smeul·trohn wild strawberry
småbröd smoa·brurd roll
småkaka smoa·kah·ka cookie [biscuit]
smårätt smoa·rairt snack
småsill smoa·sihl herring
smör smur butter
smördeg smur·deeg pastry
smörgås smur·goas Swedish open-faced sandwich
snigel sneeg·ehl snail
socker soh·kehr sugar
sockerdricka soh·kehr·drih·ka lemonade
sockerkaka soh·kehr·kah·ka sponge cake
sockerärta soh·kehr·air·ta sugar snap pea [mangetout]
sodavatten soa·da·va·tehrn soda water
soppa sohp·a soup
S.O.S. (smör, ost och sill) ehs oa ehs (smur oast ohk sihl) small plate of marinated herring, bread, butter and cheese
sparris spar·ihs asparagus
sparrissoppa spa·rihs·sohp·a asparagus soup
specialitet för landsdelen speh·sih·ahl·ih·teet furr lands·deel·ehn local specialty
spenat speh·naht spinach
spenatsoppa speh·naht·sohp·a spinach soup
sprit spreet spirits
spädgris spaird·grees unweaned piglet

squash skoawsh	squash (vegetable)
stark stark	strong (flavor)
starkt kryddad starkt krew·dad	hot (spicy)
stek steek	roast
stekt fisk steekt fisk	fried fish
stekt kyckling steekt chewk·lihng	fried chicken (not breaded)
stekt potatis steekt poa·tah·tihs	sautéed potato
stekt ägg steekt ehg	fried egg
strömming strurm·ihng	sprats (small Baltic herring)
strömmingsflundra strurm·ihngs·fleun·dra	Baltic herring, filleted and sandwiched in pairs, fried, with dill and butter filling
stuvad abborre steu·vad a·bohr·er	perch poached with onion, parsley and lemon
sufflé suh·fleh	soufflé
sultana suhl·tahn·a	sultana raisin
sur seur	sour
svamp svamp	mushroom
svart vinbär svart veen·bair	black currant
svecia sveh·see·a	semi-hard cheese
svensk punsch sven·sk peunsh	Swedish punch (sweet liqueur)
sylt sewlt	jam
sås soas	sauce
sötningsmedel surt·nihngs·mee·dehl	artificial sweetener
sötpotatis surt·poa·tah·tihs	sweet potato

sötsur sås surt·seur soas	sweet-and-sour sauce
sött suht	sweet
T-benstek tee·been·steek	T-bone steak
thé tee	tea
timjan tihm·yan	thyme
toast skagen toast skah·gehn	toast with chopped shrimp in mayonnaise, topped with bleak roe
tomat toa·maht	tomato
tomater och lök toa·mah·ter ohk lurk	tomato and onion salad
tomatjuice toa·maht·yoas	tomato juice
tomatsoppa toa·maht·soh·pa	tomato soup
tomatsås toa·maht·soas	tomato sauce
tonfisk toan·fihsk	tuna
tonic toh·nihk	tonic water
torkade dadel tohr·ka·der dah·dehl	dried date
torkade fikon tohr·ka·der fee·kohn	dried fig
torrt tohrt	dry
torsk torshk	cod
tunga tuhng·a	tongue (cow)
tunn sås tuhnn soas	light (sauce)
tunnbröd tuhnn·brurd	Swedish flat bread, can be soft or crispy
tårta toarta	sponge-based fruit or cream cake
ugnsbakad fisk eungns·bah·kad fihsk	oven-baked fish
ugnsstekt kyckling eungn·steekt chewk·lihng	roast chicken

ugnsstekt potatis eungn·steekt poa·tah·tihs	roast potato
utan koffein eu·tan ko·feen	decaffeinated
vaktel vak·tehl	quail
valfria tillbehör vahl·free·a tihl·beh·hurr	choice of side dishes
valnöt vahl·nurt	walnut
vanilj va·nihly	vanilla
vaniljsås va·nihly·soas	vanilla sauce, often like custard
varmchoklad varm shoa·klahd	hot chocolate
varmkorv varm kohrv	hot dog
varmrätt varm·rairt	warm meal, usually main course
varmt varmt	hot
vatten va·tehrn	water
vattenkrasse va·tehrn·kra·ser	watercress
vaxböna vax·bur·na	butter bean
vegetarisk meny vehg·eh·tah·risk meh·neu	vegetarian menu
vermouth vehr·meutt	vermouth
vetemjöl vee·teh·mjurl	wheat flour (regular)
whisky vihs·kee	whisky
wienerbröd vee·nehr·brurd	Danish pastry
wienerschnitzel vee·nehr·shniht·sehl	breaded veal cutlet
vild champinjon vihl·da sham·pihn·yoan	wild mushroom
vildand vihld·and	wild duck
vilt vihlt	game
viltpastej vihlt·pa·stay	game pâté
vin veen	wine
vinaigrettesås vih·neh·greht·soas	vinaigrette [French dressing]

vinbär veen·bair	currant
vindruva veen·dreu·va	grape
vinlista veen·lihs·ta	wine list
vispgrädde visp·greh·der	whipped cream
vit sås veet soas	white sauce
vitkål veet·koal	white cabbage
vitkålssallad veet·koal·sal·ad	coleslaw
vitling veet·lihng	whiting
vitlök veet·lurk	garlic
vitlöksmajonnäs veet·lurks·may·oa·nairs	garlic mayonnaise
vitlökssås veet·lurk·soas	garlic sauce
vitt viht	white (wine)
vitt bröd viht brurd	white bread
vodka vod·ka	vodka
vol au vent vohl·oa·vahnt	vol-au-vent (pastry filled with meat or fish)
våffla (med sylt och grädde) vohf·la meed sewlt ohk greh·der	waffle (with jam and whipped cream)
vårlök voar lurk	shallot [spring onion]
västerbotten vehs·tehr·boh·tehn	strong, tangy, hard cheese
västkustsallad vehst·kuhst·sal·ad	west coast salad, with shrimp [prawns] and mussels
yoghurt yoa·geurt	yogurt
zucchini seu·kee·nee	zucchini [courgette]
ål oal	eel
ångkokt fisk oang·koakt fisk	steamed fish

ädelost air·dehl·oast	blue cheese
ägg ehg	egg
äggplanta ehg·plan·ta	eggplant [aubergine]
äggula ehg·geu·la	egg yolk
äggröra ehg·rur·ra	scrambled egg
äggvita ehg·vee·ta	egg white
älg ehly	moose
älgfilé ehly·fih·leh	fillet of moose
älgstek ehly·steek	moose roast
älgstek med svampsås ehly·steek meed svamp·soas	roast moose with mushroom sauce
äppelkaka eh·pehl·kah·ka	apple cake
äppelpaj ehp·ehl·pay	apple tart
äppelring ehp·ehl·rihng	apple fritter
äpple ehp·leh	apple
ärta air·ta	pea
ärtsoppa airt·sohp·a	green or yellow pea soup
ättiksgurka eh·tihks·geur·ka	sweet, pickled gherkins
öl url	beer
öl på flaska url poa fla·ska	bottled beer

People

Talking

Essential

Hello!	**Hej!** hay
How are you?	**Hur står det till?** heur stoar dee tihl
Fine, thanks. And you?	**Bra, tack. Och du?** brah tak ohk deu
Excuse me!	**Ursäkta!** eur•shehk•ta
Do you speak English?	**Talar du engelska?** tah•lar deu ehng•ehl•ska
What's your name?	**Vad heter du?** vahd hee•tehr deu
My name is…	**Jag heter…** yahg hee•tehr…
Nice to meet you.	**Trevligt att träffas.** treev•lihgt at trehf•as
Where are you from?	**Var kommer du ifrån?** vahr ko•mehr deu ee•froan
I'm from the *U.S./U.K.*	**Jag kommer från *USA/Storbritannien.*** yahg koh•mehr froan *eu ehs ah/ stoar•bree•tan•yehn*
What do you do?	**Vad sysslar du med?** vahd sews•lar deu meed
I work for…	**Jag jobbar på…** yahg yohb•ar poa…
I'm a student.	**Jag är student.** yahg air stuh•dent
I'm retired.	**Jag är pensionär.** yahg air pang•shoa•nair
Do you like…?	**Tycker du om…?** tew•kehr deu ohm…
Goodbye.	**Hej då.** hay•doa
See you later.	**Vi ses.** vee sees

Communication Difficulties

Do you speak English?	**Talar du engelska?** tah·lar deu ehng·ehl·ska
Does anyone here speak English?	**Talar någon engelska här?** tah·lar noa·gohn ehng·ehl·ska hair
I don't speak Swedish.	**Jag talar inte svenska.** yahg tah·lar ihn·ter svehn·ska
Could you speak more slowly?	**Kan du tala lite långsammare?** kan deu tah·la lee·ter loang·sam·a·rer
Could you repeat that?	**Kan du upprepa det?** kan deu uhp·ree·pah dee
Excuse me?	**Ursäkta?** eur·shehk·ta
What was that?	**Vad var det?** vahd vahr dee
Write it down, please.	**Skriv ner det, tack.** skreev neer dee tak
Can you translate this for me?	**Kan du översätta det här?** kan deu ur·ver·seh·ta deet hair
What does *this/that* mean?	**Vad betyder det *här/där*?** vad beh·tew·der dee *hair/dair*
I understand.	**Jag förstår.** yahg furr·stoar
I don't understand.	**Jag förstår inte.** yahg furr·stoar ihn·ter
Do you understand?	**Förstår du?** furr·stoar deu

You May Hear...

Jag talar bara lite engelska. yahg tah·lar bah·ra lee·ter ehng·ehl·ska	I speak only a little English.
Jag talar inte engelska. yahg tah·lar in·ter ehng·ehl·ska	I don't speak English.

Making Friends

Hello.	**Hej.** hay
Good morning.	**God morgon.** goad mor·on

Good afternoon.	**God middag.** goad mi·dahg
Good evening.	**God afton.** goad af·tohn
My name is…	**Jag heter…** yahg hee·tehr…
What's your name?	**Vad heter du?** vahd hee·tehr deu
I'd like to introduce you to…	**Får jag presentera…** foar yahg preh·sehn·tee·ra…
Pleased to meet you.	**Trevligt att träffas.** treev·lihgt at treh·fas
How are you?	**Hur står det till?** heur stoar dee tihl
Fine, thanks.	**Bra, tack.** brah tak
And you?	**Och du?** ohk deu

Swedes shake hands when greeting someone and when saying goodbye; this holds for meeting new people but is also often the case with colleagues or acquaintances. When you meet someone for the first time, shake hands and give your name. As in many countries, titles are more commonly used by the older generation, but you will sometimes hear **herr** (Mr.), **fru** (Mrs.) and **fröken** (Miss) used, as well as professional titles, e.g., **doktor** (doctor), **ingenjör** (engineer), etc.

Travel Talk

I'm here...	**Jag är här...** yahg air hair...
– on business	**– på affärsresa** poa a·fairs·ree·sa
– on vacation [holiday]	**– på semester** poa seh·mehs·tehr
– studying	**– för studier** furr steu·de·ehr
I'm staying for...	**Jag ska stanna i...** yahg skah sta·na ee...
I've been here...	**Jag har varit här i...** yahg hahr vah·riht hair ee...
– a day	**– en dag** ehn dahg
– a week	**– en vecka** ehn veh·ka
– a month	**– en månad** ehn moa·nad

▶ For numbers, see page 184.

Where are you from?	**Var kommer du ifrån?** vahr koh·mehr deu ee·froan
I'm from...	**Jag kommer från...** yahg koh·mehr froan...

Relationships

Who are you here with?	**Vem är du här med?** vehm air deu hair meed
I'm on my own.	**Jag är ensam.** yahg air ehn·sam
I'm with...	**Jag är här med...** yahg air hair meed...
– my *husband/wife*	**– min *man/fru*** mihn *man/freu*
– my *boyfriend/ girlfriend*	**– min *pojkvän/flickvän*** mihn *poyk·vehn/ flihk·vehn*
– a friend/friends	**– en vän/vänner** ehn vehn/venhn·ehr
– a colleague/ colleagues	**– en kollega/kolleger** ehn koh·lee·ga/ koh·lee·goahr

When's your birthday?	**När fyller du år?** nair <u>fewl</u>·ehr deu **oa**r
How old are you?	**Hur gammal är du?** heur <u>gah</u>·mal air deu

▶ For numbers, see page 184.

I'm…	**Jag är…** yahg air…
– single	**– ogift** <u>oa</u>·yift
– in a relationship	**– i ett förhållande** ee eht furr·<u>hoal</u>·an·der
– married	**– gift** yihft
– divorced	**– skild** shihld
– separated	**– separerad** seh·pa·<u>ree</u>·rad
I'm a *widow/widower.*	**Jag är *änka/änkling.*** yahg air *<u>ehng</u>·ka/ <u>ehngk</u>·lihng*
Do you have *children/ grandchildren*?	**Har du *barn/barnbarn*?** hahr deu *bahrn/ <u>bahrn</u>·bahrn*

Work and School

What do you do?	**Vad sysslar du med?** vahd <u>sews</u>·lar deu meed
What are you studying?	**Vad läser du?** vahd <u>lai</u>·sehr deu
I'm studying…	**Jag läser…** yahg <u>lai</u>·sehr…
Who do you work for?	**Vilken firma jobbar du på?** <u>vihl</u>·kehn <u>fihr</u>·ma <u>yohb</u>·ar deu p**oa**
I work for…	**Jag jobbar på…** yahg <u>yohb</u>·ar p**oa**…
Here's my business card.	**Här är mitt kort.** hair air miht koahrt

▶ For business travel, see page 160.

Weather

What's the weather forecast for tomorrow?	**Vad är väderleksrapporten för imorgon?** vahd air vair·dehr·leeks·ra·pohr·tehn furr ee·mo·ron
What *beautiful/terrible* weather!	**Vilket *vackert/förskräckligt* väder!** vihl·keht *va·kert/furr·skrehk·ligt* vair·dehr
It's...	**Det är...** dee air...
– cool/warm	**– svalt/varmt** svahlt/varmt
– rainy/sunny	**– regnigt/soligt** rehng·nihkt/soal·ikt
– snowy/icy	**– snöigt/halt** snur·ikt/hahlt
Do I need *a jacket/an umbrella*?	**Behöver jag *en jacka/ett paraply*?** beh·hur·ver yahg *ehn yah·ka/eht pa·ra·plew*

▶ For temperature, see page 190.

Romance

Essential

Would you like to go out for *a drink/dinner*?	**Har du lust att *ta en drink/gå ut och äta?*** hahr deu luhst at *tah ehn drihnk/goa eut ohk air·ta*
What are your plans for *tonight/tomorrow*?	**Vad har du för planer för *ikväll/imorgon*?** vahd hahr deu furr plah·nehr furr *ee·kvehl/ee·mo·ron*
Can I have your number?	**Kan jag få ditt telefonnummer?** kan yahg foa diht teh·leh·foan·nuhm·ehr
May I join you?	**Får jag göra dig sällskap?** foar yahg yurra dihg sehl·skahp
Can I buy you a drink?	**Får jag bjuda på en drink?** foar yahg byeu·da poa ehn drihnk
I like you.	**Jag gillar dig.** yahg yihl·ar day
I love you.	**Jag älskar dig.** yahg ehl·skar day

Making Plans

Would you like to…?	**Har du lust att…?** hahr deu luhst at…
– go out for coffee	**– gå ut och ta en kopp kaffe** goa eut ohk tah ehn kohp ka•fer
– go for a drink	**– ta en drink** tah ehn drihnk
– go out for a meal	**– gå ut och äta** goa eut ohk air•ta
What are your plans for…?	**Vad har du för planer för…?** vahd hahr deu furr plah•nehr furr…
– tonight	**– ikväll** ee•kvehl
– tomorrow	**– imorgon** ee•mo•ron
– this weekend	**– den här helgen** dehn hair hehl•yehn
Where would you like to go?	**Vart vill du gå?** vart vihl deu goa
I'd like to go to…	**Jag skulle vilja gå till…** yahg skuh•ler vihl•ya goa tihl…
Do you like…?	**Tycker du om…?** tew•kehr deu ohm…
Can I have your *number/e-mail*?	**Kan jag få *ditt nummer/din e-post*?** kan yahg foa *diht nuhm•ehr/dihn ee•pohst*

▶ For e-mail and phone, see page 49.

Pick-up [Chat-up] Lines

Can I join you?	**Får jag följa med?** foar yahg furl·ya meed
You look great!	**Vad du ser vacker ut!** vahd deu seer va·kehr eut
Shall we go somewhere quieter?	**Ska vi gå till ett lugnare ställe?** skah vee goa tihl eht luhng·na·rer stehl·ler

Accepting and Rejecting

Thank you. I'd love to.	**Tack, det vill jag gärna.** tak dee vihl yahg yair·na
Where should we meet?	**Var ska vi träffas?** vahr skah vee treh·fas
I'll meet you at *the bar/your hotel*.	**Vi träffas *i baren/på ditt hotell*.** vee treh·fas *ee bahr·en/poa diht hoh·tehl*
I'll come by at…	**Jag kommer…** yahg koh·mehr…
Thank you, but I'm busy.	**Tack, men jag är upptagen.** tak men yahg air uhp·tah·gehn
I'm not interested.	**Jag är inte intresserad.** yahg air in·ter in·treh·see·rad
Leave me alone, please!	**Kan du lämna mig ifred, tack!** kan deu lehm·na may ee·freed tak
Stop bothering me!	**Sluta störa mig!** sluh·ta stur·ra may

Getting Physical

Can I *hug/kiss* you?	**Får jag *krama/kysa* dig?** foar yahg *krah·ma/chews·a* day
Yes.	**Ja.** yah
No.	**Nej.** nay
Stop!	**Stopp!** stop

Sexual Preferences

Are you gay?	**Är du gay?** air deu gay
I'm…	**Jag är…** yahg air…
– heterosexual	**– heterosexuell** heh·tehr·ro·sehk·shew·ehl
– homosexual	**– homosexuell** hoh·moa·sehk·shew·ehl
– bisexual	**– bisexuell** bee·sehk·shew·ehl

▶ For informal and formal "you," see page 180.

▼ Fun

Sightseeing

Essential

Where's the tourist information office?	**Var ligger turistinformationen?** vahr lih•gehr teu•rihst•ihn•fohr•ma•shoan•ehn
What are the main points of interest?	**Vad finns det för sevärdheter?** vahd fihns dee furr see•vaird•hee•tehr
Do you have tours in English?	**Finns det några turer på engelska?** fihns dee noa•gra teu•rehr poa ehng•ehl•ska
Can I have a *map/guide*, please?	**Kan jag få en *karta/guide*, tack?** kan yahg foa ehn *kahr•ta/gujd* tak

Tourist Information Office

Do you have any information on...?	**Har ni information om...?** hahr nee ihn•for•ma•shoan om...
Can you recommend...?	**Kan ni rekommendera...?** kan nee reh•koh•mehn• dee•ra...
– a boat trip	**– en båttur** ehn boat•teur
– an excursion	**– en rundtur** ehn ruhnd•teur
– a sightseeing tour	**– en sightseeingtur** ehn sight•see•ihng•teur

There are tourist information offices in all large cities and towns. These are usually marked by a green sign with an **I**. For general information, Sweden's official tourism website is a good place to start. Here you can find information on accommodation, attractions and activities as well as cultural and historical information. Most cities have their own tourist boards and websites, where you can request brochures, maps and more prior to your arrival. Also look for **Stockholmskortet** (the Stockholm Card) if you will be spending several days in the city. For one fee, you have access to musems, events and transportation throughout the city. You can choose whether you want the card for 24, 48 or 72 hours. The equivalent in Göteborg is **Göteborgs Passet.**

▶For useful websites, see page 191.

Tours

I'd like to go on the tour to...	**Jag vill följa med på turen till...** yahg vihl furl·ja meed poa teu·ren tihl...
Are there tours in English?	**Finns det någon tur på engelska?** fihns dee noa·gohn teur poa ehng·ehl·ska
What time do we *leave/return*?	**När *åker vi/kommer vi tillbaka*?** nair *oak·er vee/koh·mehr vee tihl·bah·ka*
We'd like to have a look at...	**Vi skulle vilja se...** vee skuh·ler vihl·ya see...
Can we stop here...?	**Kan vi stanna här...?** kan vee sta·na hair...
– to take photographs	**– för att ta foton** furr at tah foa·tohn
– to buy souvenirs	**– för att köpa souvenirer** furr at chur·pa seu·veh·nee·rehr
– to use the restroom [toilet]	**– för att gå på toaletten** furr at goa poa toa·ah·leh·tehn
Is there access for the disabled?	**Finns det tillgång för rörelsehindrade?** fihns dee tihl·goang furr rurr·ehl·ser·hihn·dra·der

▶For ticketing, see page 21.

Sights

Where is...?	**Var ligger...?** vahr lih·gehr...
– the battleground	**– slagfältet** slahg·fehl·teht
– the botanical garden	**– botaniska trädgården** boa·tan·ihs·ska traird·goar·dehn

Where is…? **Var ligger…?** vahr lih·gehr…

– the castle **– slottet** sloht·eht

– the downtown area **– centrum** sehn·truhm

– the fountain **– fontänen** fohn·tairn·ehn

– the library **– biblioteket** bihb·lee·oa·teek·eht

– the market **– torget** tohr·yeht

– the museum **– museet** muh·see·eht

– the old town **– gamla stan** gam·la stahn

– the palace **– slottet** sloht·eht

– the park **– parken** park·ehn

– the shopping area **– Et affärscentrumet** eht a·ffairs·sehn·truhm·eht

– the town hall **– stadshuset** stads·heus·eht

Can you show me on the map?	**Kan du visa mig på kartan?** kan deu vee·sa may poa kahr·tan

▶For directions, see page 35.

Impressions

It's…	**Det är…** det air…
– beautiful	**– vackert** va·kehrt
– boring	**– trist** trihst
– interesting	**– intressant** in·treh·sant
– magnificent	**– storslaget** stoar·slahg·eht
– romantic	**– romantiskt** roh·man·tihskt
– terrible	**– hemskt** hehmskt
– ugly	**– fult** feult
I (don't) like it.	**Jag tycker (inte) om *den/det*.** yahg tew·kehr (in·ter) ohm *dehn/dee*

▶For usage of **den** and **det**, see page 183.

Religion

Where is…?	**Var är…?** vahr air…
– the church	**– kyrkan** chewr·kan
– the mosque	**– moskén** mos·kehn
– the shrine	**– altaret** alt·a·reht
– the synagogue	**– synagogan** sihn·a·gohg·an
– the temple	**– templet** tehmp·leht
What time is *mass/the service*?	**Hur dags är *mässan/gudstjänsten*?** heur daks air *mehs·an/geuds·tjain·stehn*

Shopping

Essential

Where is the *market/ mall [shopping centre]*?	**Var ligger *torget/affärscentrumet*?** vahr lih•gehr *tohr•yeht/a•ffairs•sehn•truhm•eht*
I'm just looking.	**Jag tittar bara.** yahg tih•tar bah•ra
Can you help me?	**Kan du hjälpa mig?** kan deu yehlp•a may
I'm being helped.	**Jag får hjälp, tack.** yahg foar yehlp tak
How much does it cost?	**Hur mycket kostar det?** heur mew•ker kos•tar det
This/That one, thanks.	**Den *här/där*, tack.** dehn *hair/dair* tak
That's all, thanks.	**Det var allt, tack.** dee vahr alt tak
Where do I pay?	**Var kan jag betala?** vahr kan yahg beh•tah•la
I'll pay *in cash/by credit card.*	**Jag vill betala *kontant/med kreditkort*.** yahg vihl beh•tah•la *kohn•tant/meed kreh•deet•koart*
A receipt, please.	**Kvittot, tack.** kvih•tot tak

Although Sweden still has many small, specialty shops, **Köpcentrum** (malls) are becoming more and more common, especially in larger towns. Many chain and department stores, such as **Åhléns** and **Kappahl** and **Hennes & Mauritz**, have branches all over the country, all of which sell quality goods. In the well-established Stockholm department store **NK**, you can find almost anything, though it can be quite expensive. Designer goods can be found at **DesignTorget** in Stockholm. For traditional handicrafts look for signs with **hemslöjd** (handicraft); in Stockholm, these can be found at **Svensk Hemslöjd** and **Svenskt Hantverk** (traditional handicraft stores). Many towns have colorful markets, where you can buy anything from fresh fruit and vegetables to flowers and handicrafts. **Julmarknaden** (Christmas market) in Stockholm in the Old Town and **Skansen** (outdoor park and museum), are historic shopping areas.

Stores

Where is...? **Var finns...?** vahr fihns...

- the antiques store – **antikaffären** an·teek·a·ffair·ehn
- the bakery – **bageriet** bahg·eh·ree·eht
- the bookstore – **bokhandeln** boak·han·dehln
- the clothing store – **klädaffären** klaird·a·ffair·ehn
- the delicatessen – **delikatessaffären** dehl·eh·ka·tehs·a·fair·ehn
- the department store – **varuhuset** vahr·eu·heus·eht
- the health food store – **hälsokostaffären** hehl·soa·kost·a·fair·ehn
- the jeweler – **juveleraren** yeu·veh·lee·rar·ehn
- the liquor store [off–licence] – **systembolaget** sews·teem·boa·lahg·eht
- the market – **torget** tohr·yeht
- the pastry shop – **konditoriet** kohn·deh·toh·ree·eht
- the pharmacy [chemist] – **apoteket** a·poa·tee·keht
- the produce [grocery] store – **livsmedelsaffären** lihvs·mee·dehls·a·fair·ehn
- the shoe store – **skoaffären** skoa·a·fair·ehn
- the shopping mall [shopping centre] – **affärscentrumet** a·ffairs·sehn·truhm·eht
- the souvenir store – **souvenirbutiken** seu·veh·neer·buh·tee·kehn
- the supermarket – **snabbköpet** snab·chur·peht

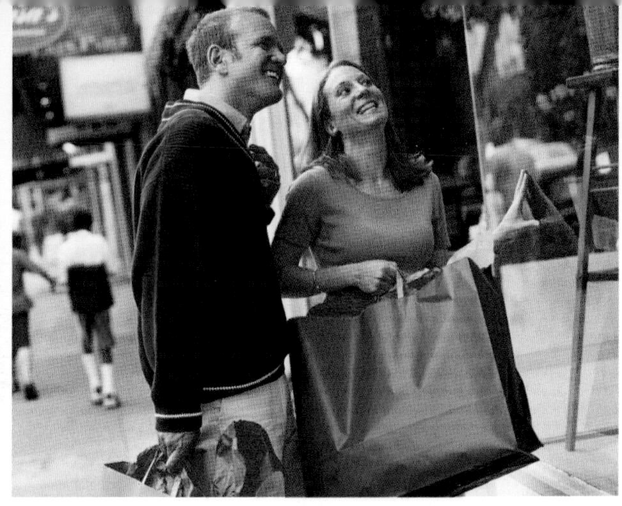

Where is...?	**Var finns...?** vahr fihns...
– the tobacconist	**– tobaksaffären** toa·baks·a·ffair·ehn
– the toy store	**– leksaksaffären** leek·sahks·a·fair·ehn

Services

Can you recommend...?	**Kan du rekommendera...?** kan deu reh·koh·mehn·dee·ra...
– a barber	**– en herrfrisör** ehn hair·fri·surr
– a dry cleaner	**– en kemtvätt** ehn shehm·tveht
– a hairdresser	**– en damfrisör** ehn dahm·free·surr
– a laundromat [launderette]	**– en snabbtvätt** ehn snab·tveht
– a nail salon	**– en nagelvårdssalong** ehn nah·gehl·voards·sa·loang
– a spa	**– ett spa** eht spah
– a travel agency	**– en resebyrå** ehn ree·seh·bew·roa

Can you...this?	**Kan ni...den här?** kan nee...dehn hair
– alter	**– ändra på** ehn•dra poa
– clean	**– göra ren** yur•ra reen
– mend	**– laga** lah•ga
– press	**– stryka** strew•ka
When will it be ready?	**När blir det klart?** nair bleer dee klahrt

Spa

I'd like...	**Jag skulle vilja ha...** yahg skuh•ler vihl•ya hah...
– an eyebrow/a bikini wax	**– en vaxning av *ögonbrynen/ bikinilinjen*** ehn vaks•nihng afv *ur•gonn•brew•nehn/beh•kee•nee•leen•yehn*
– a facial	**– en ansiktsbehandling** ehn an•sihkts•beh•hand•lihng
– a *manicure/pedicure*	**– en *manikyr/pedikyr*** ehn *ma•nee•kewr/ pehd•ee•kewr*
– a (sports) massage	**– (tränings) massage** (trair•nihngs•) ma•sahsh
Do you do...?	**Ger ni...?** yehr nee...
– acupuncture	**– akupunktur** a•keu•puhnk•teur
– aromatherapy	**– aroma-terapi** a•roa•ma•teh•ra•pee
– oxygen treatment	**– syrebehandling** sew•reh•beh•hand•lihng
Is there a sauna?	**Finns det bastu?** fihns dee bas•teu

Spas and wellness centers are becoming increasingly popular. There are many to choose from, both in urban and rural areas. It is possible to find spas that offer everything from traditional massage, such as the Swedish massage, which focuses on circulation and relaxation, to yoga, exercise and more. Some are even eco-friendly. Many spas and health centers also have gyms, pools, saunas.

Hair Salon

I'd like…	**Jag vill…** yahg vihl…
– an appointment for *today/tomorrow*	**– boka en tid till *idag/imorgon*** boa•ka ehn teed tihl *ee•dahg/ee•mo•ron*
– my hair styled	**– få en ny frisyr** foa ehn new free•sewr
– a hair cut	**– få en klippning** foa ehn klihp•nihng
Don't cut it too short.	**Klipp det inte för kort.** klihp dee ihn•ter furr koart
Shorter here.	**Kortare här.** koar•ta•rer hair

Sales Help

When do you *open/ close*?	**När *öppnar/stänger* ni?** nair *uhp•nar/ stehng•er* nee
Where is…?	**Var finns…?** vahr fihns…
– the cashier [cash desk]	**– kassan** kah•san
– the escalator	**– rulltrappan** ruhl•tra•pan
– the elevator [lift]	**– hissen** his•ehn
– the fitting room	**– provrummet** proav•ruhm•eht
– the store directory [guide]	**– informationen** in•for•ma•shoa•nehn
Can you help me?	**Kan du hjälpa mig?** kan deu yehl•pa may
I'm just looking.	**Jag tittar bara.** yahg tih•tar bah•ra
I'm being helped.	**Tack, jag får hjälp.** tak yahg foar yehlp
Do you have any…?	**Har ni några…?** hahr nee noa•gra…
Could you show me…?	**Kan du visa mig några…?** kan deu vee•sa may noa•gra…

Can you *ship/wrap* it?	**Kan du *skicka/slå in* det?** kan deu *shih·ka dee/sloa ihn* dee
How much does it cost?	**Hur mycket kostar det?** heur mew·kerht kos·tar dee
That's all, thanks.	**Det var allt, tack.** dee vahr alt tak

▶For clothing items, see page 144.

▶For food items, see page 95.

▶For souvenirs, see page 141.

You May Hear...

Kan jag hjälpa er? kan yahg yehl·pa ehr	Can I help you?
Ett ögonblick, tack. eht ur·gohn·blihk tak	Just a moment, please.
Vad vill ni beställa? vahd vihl nee beh·steh·la	What would you like?
Något annat? noa·goht an·nat	Anything else?

Preferences

I want something...	**Jag skulle vilja ha något...** yahg skuh·ler vihl·ya hah noa·goht...
– cheap/expensive	**– billigt/dyrt** bihl·igt/dewyt
– larger/smaller	**– större/mindre** sturr·er/mihn·drer
Is it real?	**Är den äkta?** air dehn aik·ta
Could you show me *this/that*?	**Kan du visa mig den *här/där*?** kan deu vee·sa may dehn *hair/dair*

Decisions

That's not quite what I want.	**Det är inte riktigt vad jag vill ha.** dee air ihn·ter rihk·tikt vahd yahg vihl hah
I don't like it.	**Jag tycker inte om det.** yahg tew·kehr ihn·ter ohm dee
That's too expensive.	**Det är för dyrt.** dee air furr dewrt
I'd like to think about it.	**Jag behöver tänka på det.** yahg beh·hur·vehr tehng·ka poa dee
I'll take it.	**Jag tar den.** yahg tahr dehn

Bargaining

That's too much.	**Det är för mycket.** dee air furr mew·ker
I'll give you…	**Jag kan ge er…** yahg kan yee ehr…
I only have…kronor.	**Jag har bara…kronor.** yahg hahr bah·ra… kroa·nohr
Can you give me a discount?	**Kan du ge mig rabatt?** kan deu yee may ra·bat

▶For numbers, see page 184.

Paying

How much does it cost?	**Hur mycket kostar det?** heur mew·ker kos·tar dee
I'll pay…	**Jag betalar…** yahg beh·tah·lar…
– in cash	**– kontant** kohn·tant
– by credit card	**– med kreditkort** meed kreh·deet·koart
– by traveler's check [cheque]	**– med en resecheck** meed ehn ree·seh·shehk
The receipt, please.	**Kvittot, tack.** kvih·toht tak

You May Hear...

Hur vill ni betala? heur vihl nee beh•tah•la	How are you paying?
Bara kontanter, tack. bah•ra kohn•tan•tehr tak	Cash only, please.
Har du mindre växel? hahr deu mihn•drer vehx•ehl	Do you have any smaller change?

Complaints

I'd like...	**Jag skulle vilja...** yahg skuh•ler vihl•ya...
– to exchange this	**– byta den här** bew•ta dehn hair
– to return this	**– återlämna den här** oa•tehr•lehm•na dehn hair
– a refund	**– ha pengarna tillbaka** hah pehng•ar•na tihl•bah•ka
– to see the manager	**– få träffa butikschefen** foa treh•fa beu•teeks•sheef•ehn

Souvenirs

candlesticks	**ljusstakar** yeus•stah•kar
Christmas decorations	**juldekorationer** yeul•dehk•oh•ra•shoan•ehr
clogs	**träskor** trair•skoar
crystal (glass)	**kristallglas** kree•stal•glahs
a Dala horse (red wooden horse)	**en dalahäst** ehn dah•la•hehst
dolls	**dockor** dok•oar
glassware	**glasföremål** glahs•furr•reh•moal
handicrafts	**hemslöjd** hehm•sluhyd
horn work	**något i horn** noa•goht ee hoarn
jewelry	**smycken** smew•kehn

porcelain	**porslin** pohrsh·<u>leen</u>
pottery	**keramik** cheh·ra·<u>meek</u>
reindeer antlers	**renhorn** <u>reen</u>·hoarn
Sami handicrafts	**sameslöjd** <u>sah</u>·meh·sluhyd
smoked salmon	**rökt lax** rurkt lax
a tablecloth	**en duk** ehn deuk
textiles	**textil** tehx·<u>teel</u>
wood carvings	**träfigurer** trair·fih·<u>geu</u>·rehr
a wooden knife	**en träkniv** ehn <u>trair</u>·kneev
a wooden spoon	**en träsked** ehn <u>trair</u>·sheed
Can I see *this/that*?	**Får jag se på den *här/där*?** foar yahg seh poa dehn *hair/dair*
The one in the *window/display case*.	**Den i *fönstret/vitrinet*.** dehn ee *<u>furn</u>·streht/ vi·<u>treen</u>·eht*
I'd like…	**Jag skulle vilja ha…** yahg <u>skuh</u>·ler <u>vihl</u>·ya hah…
– a battery	**– ett batteri** eht ba·teh·<u>ree</u>
– a bracelet	**– ett armband** eht <u>arm</u>·band
– a brooch	**– en brosch** ehn broash
– earrings	**– örhängen** <u>ur</u>·hehng·ehn
– a necklace	**– ett halsband** eht <u>hals</u>·band
– a ring	**– en ring** ehn rihng
– a watch	**– en armbandsklocka** ehn <u>arm</u>·bands·<u>kloh</u>·ka
– copper	**– koppar** <u>kohpp</u>·ar
– crystal (quartz)	**– kristall** krihs·<u>tall</u>
– diamond	**– diamant** dee·a·<u>mant</u>
– *white/yellow* gold	**– *vitt/rött* guld** *viht/rurtt* geuld
– pearl	**– pärla** <u>pair</u>·la

I'd like...	**Jag skulle vilja ha...** yahg skuh•ler vihl•ya hah...
– pewter	**– tenn** teen
– platinum	**– platina** plah•tee•na
– sterling silver	**– äkta silver** ehk•ta sihl•vehr
Is this real?	**Är den här äkta?** air dehn hair ehk•ta
Can you engrave it?	**Kan ni gravera den?** kan nee gra•vee•ra dehn

When it comes to souvenirs, whether you are looking for something traditional or modern, you are sure to find just the thing in Sweden. **Träslöjd** (woodwork), **hemslöjd** (handicrafts), **keramik** (ceramics) and Swedish crystal are popular, traditional souvenirs. The **dalahäst** (Dala horse) is perhaps one of the most famous and ubiquitous souvenirs; traditionally, its color is a reddish-orange, but the horses can now be found in a wide range of colors and sizes. Sweden is known for its design, which is evident in its selection of **porslin** (fine china) and ceramics. Some well-known manufacturers include **Höganäs Keramik** and **Rörstrand**, the latter being the second oldest porcelain manufacturer in Europe, founded in 1746. Sweden is also famous for its glass and crystal, both with respect to design and to quality. **Glasriket** (the kingdom of glass) located in Småland, in southeastern Sweden, has around 15 glass factories, including some of the most famous glassworks in Sweden, such as **Kosta Boda**, **Orrefors** and **Nybro**. Factory tours are often available. In addition to the traditional Swedish handicrafts mentioned above, **sameslöjd** (Sámi handicraft) is something that should not be overlooked. The Sámi are known for their beautiful crafts, which include jewelry and knives carved from reindeer antlers, jewelry made from beaded pewter and reindeer leather as well as a wide range of clothing in reindeer leather and different types of fur.

Antiques

How old is this?	**Hur gammalt är det här?** heur gam•alt air dee hair
Will I have problems with customs?	**Får jag problem i tullen?** foar yahg proa•bleem ee tuh•lehn
Is there a certificate of authenticity?	**Finns det ett äkthetsbevis?** fihns dee eht ehkt•heets•beh•vees

Clothing

I'd like…	**Jag skulle vilja ha…** yahg skuh•ler vihl•ya hah…
Can I try this on?	**Kan jag prova den här?** kan yahg proa•va dehn hair
It doesn't fit.	**Den passar inte.** dehn pas•ar ihn•ter

It's too… **Den är för…** dehn air furr…

– big **– stor** stoar

– small **– liten** lee·tehn

– short **– kort** kort

– long **– lång** loang

Do you have this in size…? **Har ni den här i storlek…?** hahr nee dehn hair ee stoar·leek…

Do you have this in a *bigger/smaller* size? **Har ni den här i *en större/en mindre* storlek?** hahr nee dehn hair ee *ehn stur·re/ehn mihn·drer* stoar·leek

▶For numbers, see page 184.

You May See…

HERRKLÄDER	men's clothing
DAMKLÄDER	women's clothing
BARNKLÄDER	children's clothing

Color

I'm looking for something in… **Jag söker något i…** yahg sur·ker noa·goht ee…

– beige **– beige** beesh

– black **– svart** svart

– blue **– blått** bloat

– brown **– brunt** breunt

– green **– grönt** grurnt

– gray **– grått** groat

– orange **– orange** oa·ransh

– pink **– rosa** roa·sa

– purple **– lila** lee·la

I'm looking for something in...	**Jag söker något i...** yahg sur·ker noa·goht ee...
– red	**– rött** ruhrt
– white	**– vitt** vit
– yellow	**– gult** geult

Clothes and Accessories

backpack	**ryggsäck** rewg·sehk
belt	**skärp** shairp
bikini	**bikini** bih·kee·nee
blouse	**blus** bleus
bra	**behå** beh·hoa
coat	**rock** rohk
dress	**klänning** klehn·ihng
hat	**hatt** hat
jacket	**jacka** ya·ka
jeans	**jeans** jeens
pajamas	**pyjamas** pew·ya·mas
pants [trousers]	**byxor** bewx·ohr
panty hose [tights]	**strumpbyxor** struhmp·bewx·ohr
purse [handbag]	**handväska** hand·vehs·ka
raincoat	**regnkappa** rehngn·kap·a
scarf	**halsduk** hals·deuk
shirt	**skjorta** shoar·ta
shorts	**shorts** shohrts
skirt	**kjol** choal
socks	**sockar** soh·kar
suit (jacket and pants)	**kostym** kos·tewm

suit (jacket and skirt) **dräkt** drehkt

sunglasses **solglasögon** soal·glahs·**ur**·gohn

sweater **tröja** trur·ya

sweatshirt **sweatshirt** sweat·shirt

swimming trunks **badbyxor** bahd·bewx·ohr

swimsuit **baddräkt** bahd·drehkt

T-shirt **T-skjorta** tee·shoarta

tie **slips** slihps

underpants (men's/women's) **kalsonger/trosor** kal·soang·ehr/troa·sohr

Fabric

I'd like... **Jag skulle vilja ha...** yahg skuh·ler vihl·ya hah...

– cotton **– bomull** boam·uhl

– denim **– denim** dehn·ihm

– lace **– spets** spehts

– leather **– läder** lair·der

– linen **– linne** lih·ner

– silk **– siden** see·dehn

– wool **– ull** uhl

Is it machine washable? **Kan det tvättas i maskin?** kan dee tveht·as ee ma·sheen

Shoes

I'd like... **Jag skulle vilja ha...** yahg skuh·ler vihl·ya hah...

– *high-heeled/flat* shoes ***– högklackade/lågklackade*** **skor** *hurg·klak·a·der/loag·klak·a·der* skoar

– boots **– stövlar** stuhv·lar

I'd like...	**Jag skulle vilja ha...** yahg skuh·ler vihl·ya hah...
– loafers	**– loafers** loa·fers
– sandals	**– sandaler** san·dahl·ehr
– shoes	**– skor** skoar
– slippers	**– tofflor** toff·lohr
– sneakers	**– träningsskor** trair·nihngs·skoar
In size...	**I storlek...** ee stoar·leek...

▶For numbers, see page 184.

Sizes

small	**liten** leet·ehn
medium	**medium** mee·dee·uhm
large	**stor** stoar
extra large	**extra stor** ehx·tra stoar
petite	**petite** peh·teet
plus size	**plus-storlek** pleus·stoar·leek

Newsstand and Tobacconist

Do you sell English-language *books/newspapers*?	**Säljer ni *böcker/tidningar* på engelska?** sehl·yehr nee *bur·kehr/teed·nihng·ar* poa ehng·ehl·ska
I'd like...	**Jag skulle vilja ha...** yahg skuh·ler vihl·ya hah...
– some chewing gum	**– tuggummi** tuhg·guh·mee
– some cigars	**– några cigarrer** noa·gra see·gahr·er
– a *pack/carton* of cigarettes	**– *ett paket/en limpa* cigaretter** *eht pak·eht/ehn lihm·pa* sih·ga·reht·ehr
– a lighter	**– en tändare** ehn tehn·da·rehr
– a magazine	**– en veckotidning** ehn veh·koa·teed·nihng

– matches	**– tändstickor** tehnd·stik·ohr
– a newspaper	**– en tidning** ehn teed·nihng
– a postcard	**– ett vykort** eht vew·koart
– a *road/town* map of...	**– en *vägkarta/stadskarta* över...** ehn *vairg·kahr·ta/stats·kahr·ta* **ur**·vehr...
– some stamps	**– några frimärken** noa·gra free·mair·kehn

Photography

I'm looking for... camera.	**Jag skulle vilja köpa...kamera.** yahg skuh·ler vihl·ya ch**ur**·pa...kah·meh·ra
– an automatic	**– en automatisk** ehn ah·toa·mah·tihsk
– a digital	**– en digital** ehn dih·gih·tahl
– a disposable	**– en engångs** ehn een·goangs
I'd like...	**Jag skulle vilja ha...** yahg skuh·ler vihl·ya hah...
– a battery	**– ett batteri** eht ba·teh·ree
– a digital print	**– ett digitalt kort** eht dih·gih·tahlt koart
– a memory card	**– ett minneskort** eht mihn·ehs·koart
Can I print digital photos here?	**Kan jag skriva ut digitala foton här?** kan yahg skree·va eut dih·gih·tah·la foh·toan hair

Sports and Leisure

Essential

When's the game?	**När börjar matchen?** nair **bur**·yar ma·shchehn
Where's...?	**Var ligger...?** vahr lih·gehr...
– the beach	**– stranden** stran·dehn

Where's…?	**Var ligger…?** vahr lih•gehr…
– the park	**– parken** park•ehn
– the pool	**– simbassängen** sihm•ba•sehng•ehn
Is it safe to *swim/dive* here?	**Kan man *simma/dyka* här utan risk?** kan man *sihmm•a/dew•ka* hair eu•tan rihsk
Can I rent [hire] golf clubs?	**Kan man hyra golfklubbor?** kan man hew•ra gohlf•kluh•bohr
How much per hour?	**Vad kostar det per timme?** vahd kos•tar dee pair tihm•er
How far is it to…?	**Hur långt är det till…?** heur loangt air dee tihl…
Can you show me on the map?	**Kan du visa mig på kartan?** kan deu vee•sa may poa kahr•tan

Spectator Sports

When's…?	**När börjar…?** nair bur•yar…
– the basketball game	**– basketbollmatchen** bahs•keht•bohl•ma•shchehn
– the cycling race	**– cykeltävlingen** sew•kehl•taiv•lihng•ehn
– the golf tournament	**– golfspelet** golf•spee•leht
– the soccer [football] game	**– fotbollsmatchen** foat•bohls•ma•shchehn
– the tennis match	**– tennismatchen** tehn•ihs•ma•shchehn
Which teams are playing?	**Vilka lag spelar?** vihl•ka lahg spee•lar
Where's the stadium?	**Var ligger idrottsarenan?** vahr lih•gehr ee•drohts•a•ree•nan
Where can I place a bet?	**Var kan jag spela lotto?** vahr kan yahg spee•la loh•toa

Sports and recreation are popular, and there are excellent sports facilities everywhere, ranging from **golf** (golf), **fiske** (fishing), **tennis** (tennis) and **fotboll** (soccer) to **skidåkning** (skiing) and **ishockey** (ice hockey). Tourist offices should have contact information for the various sports facilities in your area. Swedes also love the great outdoors, and the country has much to offer when it comes to **bergklättring** (mountain climbing), **vandring** (hiking), **ridsport** (horsebackriding), **cykelåkning** (cycling), **paddla kanot** (canoeing) and **segling** (boating). Whether you are looking for a day hike or planning a longer trip, some great choices include **Kebnekaise**, which is Sweden's highest mountain, **Kungsleden**, **Bohusleden** or **Padjelantleden**. There are a lot of options for cyclists, both amateurs and professionals, and popular cycle routes include **Kustlinjen** and **Sverigeleden**.

Participating

Is there…nearby?	**Finns det…i närheten?** fihns dee…ee nair·hee·ten
– a golf course	**– en golfbana** ehn gohlf·bah·na
– a gym	**– ett gym** eht yim
– a park	**– en park** ehn park
– a tennis court	**– en tennisbana** ehn tehn·ihs·bah·nohr

How much per…?	**Hur mycket kostar det per…?** heur mew•ker kos•tar dee pair…
– day	**– dag** dahg
– hour	**– timme** tihm•er
– game	**– spel** speel
– round	**– runda** ruhn•da
Can I rent [hire]…?	**Kan man hyra…?** kan man hew•ra…
– golf clubs	**– klubbor** kluhb•ohr
– equipment	**– utrustning** eut•ruhst•nihng
– a racket	**– en racket** ehn ra•keht

At the Beach/Pool

Where's the *beach/ pool*?	**Var är *stranden/simbassängen*?** vahr air *stran•dehn/sihm•ba•sehng•ehn*
Is there a…here?	**Finns det…här?** fihns dee…hair
– a kiddie [paddling] pool	**– en barnbassäng** ehn bahrn•bah•sehng
– an *indoor/outdoor* pool	**– en *inomhuspool/utomhuspool*** ehn *in•ohm•heus•poal/eut•ohm•heus•poal*
– a lifeguard	**– en livräddare** leev•rehd•a•rer
Is it safe to *swim/ dive*?	**Kan man *simma/dyka* här utan risk?** kan man *sihm•a/dew•ka* hair eu•tan rihsk
Is it safe for children?	**Är det barnsäkert?** air dee bahrn•sair•kert
I want to rent [hire]…	**Jag skulle vilja hyra…** yahg skuh•ker vihl•ya hew•ra…
– a deck chair	**– en solstol** ehn soal•stoal
– a jet ski	**– en jetski** ehn jeht•skee
– a motorboat	**– en motorbåt** ehn moa•tor•boat

– a rowboat	**– en roddbåt** ehn rohd·boat
– a surfboard	**– en surfbräda** ehn suhrf·brair·da
– a towel	**– en handduk** ehn hand·deuk
– an umbrella	**– en solparasol** ehn soal·pa·ra·sohl
– water skis	**– vattenskidor** va·tehrn·shee·dohr

▶For travel with children, see page 162.

A significant portion of the Swedish coastline is rough, covered with granite rocks and cliffs and dotted with beaches. Most of the sandy beaches are found in the south and on the southwest coasts. Around Stockholm you can swim and dive from the small islands in the archipelago—and you can even swim in the water around Stockholm itself. Inland lakes, coastal areas and the popular archipelagos of Stockholm and the West Coast are perfect for boaters, and canoers and kayakers alike.

Winter Sports

A lift pass for *a day/five days*, please.	**Ett liftpass *för en dag/för fem dagar*, tack.** eht lihft·pas *furr ehn dahg/furr fehm dahg·ar* tak
I'd like to rent…	**Jag skulle vilja hyra…** yahg skuh·ler vihl·ya hew·ra…
– boots	**– skidpjäxor** sheed·pyeaix·ohr
– a helmet	**– en hjälm** ehn yehlm
– poles	**– stavar** stah·var
– skis	**– skidor** shee·dohr
– a snowboard	**– en snowboard** ehn snow·board
– snowshoes	**– pjäxor** pyaix·ohr

These are too *big/ small.*	**De här är för *stora/små.*** dehm hair air f**ur**r *st**oa**·ra/sm**oa***
Are there lessons?	**Kan man få lektioner?** kan man f**oa** lehk·sh**oa**·nehr
I'm experienced.	**Jag har erfarenhet.** yahg hahr air·fah·rehn·heet
A trail [piste] map, please.	**En karta över spåren, tack.** ehn kahr·ta **ur**·vehr sp**oa**·rehn tak

Swedes grow up with skiing: cross-country in the south and downhill in the north. There are many excellent ski resorts in the north, offering superb skiing and first-class facilities. Many hotels offer three- to seven-day package deals, including transportation and accommodation. In June, try **Riksgränsen** for a taste of skiing in the midnight sun.

Långfärdsbussar (long-distance buses) are efficient, relatively cheap and run daily to all major towns and resorts. Most of the major ski resorts also offer other winter sport activities like snowmobile safaris, snowshoeing and dog sledding tours. **Ishotellet** (Ice Hotel), though not a ski resort specifically, does offer several of these activities.

You May See...

DRAGLIFT	drag lift
ÄGGLIFT	cable car
STOLLIFT	chair lift
NYBÖRJARE	novice
MELLANNIVÅ	intermediate
AVANCERAD	expert
SPÅRET STÄNGD	trail [piste] closed

In the Countryside

I'd like a map of...	**Jag skulle vilja ha en karta över...** yahg skuh·ler vihl·ya hah ehn kahr·ta **ur**·vehr...
– this region	**– denna region** dehn·a reh·gioan
– walking routes	**– vandringsleder** van·drihngs·lee·dehr
– cycle routes	**– cykeleder** sew·kehl·lee·dehr
– the trails	**– spåren** spoa·rehn
Is it *easy/difficult*?	**Är det *lätt/svårt*?** air dee *leht/svoart*
Is it *far/steep*?	**Är det *långt/brant*?** air dee *loangt/brant*
How far is it to...?	**Hur långt är det till...?** heur loangt air dee tihl...
Can you show me on the map?	**Kan du visa mig på kartan?** kan deu vee·sa may poa kahr·tan
I'm lost.	**Jag har kommit vilse.** yahg hahr koh·miht vihl·ser
Where's...?	**Var ligger...?** vahr lih·gehr...
– the bridge	**– bron** broan
– the cave	**– grottan** groht·an
– the cliff	**– klippa** klihp·an
– the farm	**– bondgården** boand·goard·ehn
– the footpath	**– fotvandringsleden** foat·vand·rihngs·lee·dehn
– the forest	**– skogen** skoag·ehn
– the lake	**– sjön** shurn
– the mountain	**– berget** behr·yeht
– the mountain pass	**– bergspasset** berys·pas·eht
– the mountain range	**– bergskedjan** berys·chee·dyan
– the nature reserve	**– naturreservatet** na·teur·res·her·vah·teht
– the panorama	**– panoraman** pan·o·rah·man
– the park	**– parken** park·ehn

Where's…?	**Var ligger…?** vahr lih•gehr…
– the *picnic area/rest area*	**– picknickområdet/rastplatsen** pihk•nihk•ohm•roa•det/rast•plats•ehn
– the peak	**– toppen** tohp•ehn
– the river	**– floden** fload•ehn
– the sea	**– havet** hafv•eht
– the valley	**– dalen** dahl•ehn
– the viewpoint	**– utsiktspunkten** eut•sihkts•peunk•tehn
– the village	**– byn** bewn
– the waterfall	**– vattenfallet** va•tehrn•fal

Culture and Nightlife

Essential

Do you have a program of events?	**Har ni ett evenemangsprogram?** hahr nee eht eh•vehn•eh•mangs•proa•gram
What's playing at the movies [cinema] tonight?	**Vad visas på bio ikväll?** vahd vee•sas poa bee•oa ee•kvehl
Where's…?	**Var ligger…?** vahr lih•gehr…
– the downtown area	**– centrum** sehn•truhm
– the bar	**– baren** bah•rehn
– the dance club	**– diskoteket** dis•koh•tee•keht

Entertainment

Can you recommend…?	**Kan du rekommendera…?** kan deu reh•koh•mehn•dee•ra…
– a concert	**– en konsert** ehn kohn•sair

– a movie	**– en film** ehn film
– an opera	**– en opera** ehn oa•peh•ra
– a play	**– en teaterpjäs** ehn tee•ah•tehr•pjais
When does it *start/ end*?	**När *börjar/slutar* den?** nair *bur•yar/sleu•tar* dehn
What's the dress code?	**Vilken klädsel gäller?** vihl•kehn klaid•sehl gehl•lehr
I like…	**Jag tycker om…** yahg tew•kehr ohm…
– classical music	**– klassisk musik** klas•isk meu•seek
– folk music	**– folkmusik** folk•meu•seek
– jazz	**– jazz** yas
– pop music	**– popmusik** pop•meu•seek
– rap	**– rap** rap

▶ For ticketing, see page 21.

Nightlife

What's there to do at night?	**Vad kan man göra på kvällarna?** vahd kan man yur•ra poa kvehl•ar•na
Can you recommend…?	**Kan du rekommendera…?** kan deu reh•koh•mehn•dee•ra…
– a bar	**– en bar** ehn bahr
– a casino	**– ett kasino** eht ka•see•noh
– a dance club	**– ett diskotek** eht dis•koh•tehk
– a gay club	**– en gayklubb** ehn gay•kluhb
– a jazz club	**– en jazzklubb** ehn yas•kluhb
– a club with local music	**– en klubb med lokal musik** ehn kluhb meed lo•kahl meu•seek
Is there live music?	**Spelar man livemusik där?** spee•lar man live•meu•seek dair

How do I get there?	**Hur kan jag komma dit?** heur kan yahg koh•ma deet
Is there a cover charge?	**Är det kuvertavgift?** air de keu•vair•afv•yihft
Let's go dancing.	**Vi går ut och dansar.** vee goar eut ohk dan•sar

i Sweden has produced several world famous pop and rock bands, and music is an important part of contemporary culture and entertainment. The government generously supports independent musicians, as well as smaller music groups, orchestras and symphonies. In larger cities and towns you'll easily find concerts and performances to attend, and information should be listed at the tourist office or its webpage regarding upcoming concerts and events. If you are traveling in Sweden during the summer, attending a music festival is an unforgettable experience. **The Peace & Love Festival** in Borlänge, just two hours from Stockholm, is popular among the younger crowd. Stockholm is home to **Ung08**, which is Europe's largest youth festival, geared toward 13–19 year olds. **The Hultsfred Festival**, in southern Sweden, is the oldest and largest festival. There are also a host of other music festivals covering everything from folk music, to pop and jazz.

You May Hear…

Stäng av mobiltelefonen, tack. stehng afv mo•beel•teh•leh•foa•nen tak	Turn off your cell [mobile] phones, please.

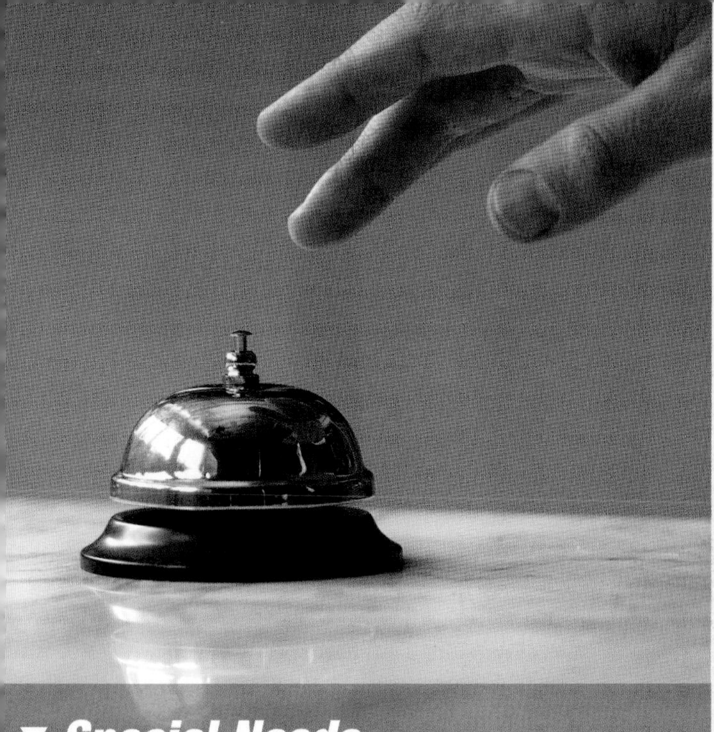

▼ Special Needs

Business Travel

Essential

I'm here on business.	**Jag är här på affärsresa.** yahg air hair poa a•fairs•ree•sa
Here's my business card.	**Här är mitt kort.** hair air miht koart
Can I have your card?	**Kan jag få ditt kort?** kan yahg foa diht koart
I have a meeting with…	**Jag har ett möte med…** yahg hahr eht mur•ter meed…
Where's…?	**Var ligger…?** vahr lih•gehr…
– the business center	**– businesscentret** bihs•nihs•sehn•treht
– the convention hall	**– kongresshallen** kohn•grehs•ha•lehn
– the meeting room	**– konferensrummet** kohn•feh•rans•ruhm•eht

Business Communication

I'm here to attend…	**Jag är här för att delta i…** yahg air hair furr at deel•tah ee…
– a seminar	**– ett seminarium** eht sehm•i•nah•ree•uhm
– a conference	**– en konferens** ehn kohn•fehr•ans
– a meeting	**– ett sammanträde** eht sam•an•trai•der
My name is…	**Jag heter…** yahg hee•ter…
May I introduce my colleague…	**Får jag presentera min kollega…** foar yahg prehs•ehn•tee•ra mihn koh•lee•ga…
Nice to meet you.	**Trevligt att träffas.** treev•ligt at trehf•as
I'm sorry I'm late.	**Ursäkta för att jag är sen.** eur•shehk•ta furr at yahg air sehn

I'd like an interpreter.	**Jag behöver en tolk.** yahg beh•hur•ver ehn tohlk
You can reach me at the…Hotel.	**Du kan nå mig på hotell…** deu kan noa may poa ho•tehl…
I'm here until…	**Jag stannar till…** yahg stan•ar tihl…
I need to…	**Jag behöver…** yahg beh•hur•ver…
– make a call	**– ringa ett samtal** rihng•a eht sam•tahl
– make a photocopy	**– göra en kopia** gur•ra ehn koh•pee•ya
– send an e-mail	**– skicka e-post** shihk•a ee•pohst
– send a fax	**– skicka en fax** shihk•a ehn fax
– send a package (overnight)	**– skicka ett paket (med expressutdelning)** shihk•a eht pa•keet (meed ehx•prehs•eut•deel•nihng)

▶For internet and communications, see page 49.

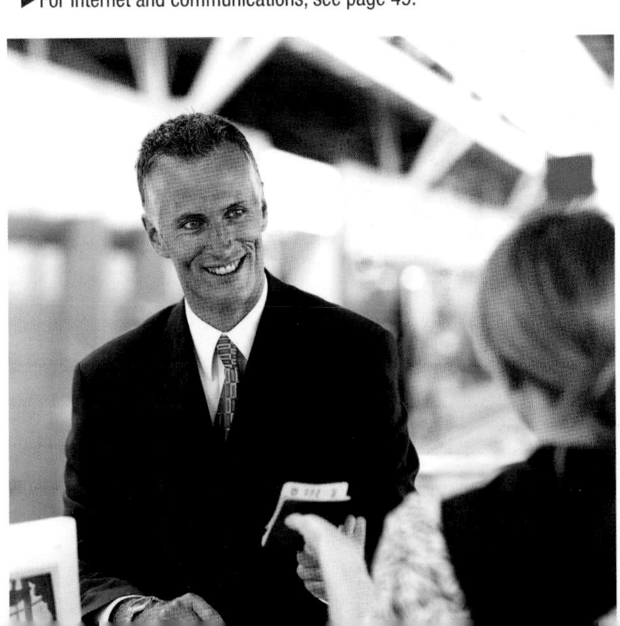

You May Hear...

Har ni bokat tid? hahr nee boa·kat teed	Do you have an appointment?
Med vem? meed vehm	With whom?
***Han/Hon* sitter i möte.** *han/hoan* sih·ter ee mur·ter	*He/She* is in a meeting.
Ett ögonblick, tack. eht ur·gohn·blik tak	One moment, please.
Tack för att ni kom. tak furr at nee kom	Thank you for coming.

Travel with Children

Essential

Is there a discount for kids?	**Har ni barnrabatt?** hahr nee bahrn·rah·bat
Can you recommend a babysitter?	**Kan du rekommendera en barnvakt?** kan deu reh·koh·mehn·dee·ra ehn bahrn·vakt
Could I have a highchair?	**Kan jag få en barnstol, tack?** kan yahg foa ehn bahrn·stoal tak
Where can I change the baby?	**Var kan jag byta på babyn?** vahr kan yahg bew·ta poa bai·been
Where's...?	**Var ligger...?** vahr lih·gehr...
– the amusement park	**– nöjesfältet** nury·ehs·fehl·teht
– the arcade	**– arkadhallen** ar·kahd·ha·lehn
– the kiddie [paddling] pool	**– barnbassängen** bahrn·ba·sehng·ehn

– the park	– **parken** park·kehn
– the playground	– **lekplatsen** leek·plats·ehn
– the zoo	– **djurparken** yeur·park·ehn
Are kids allowed?	**Får man ta barnen med?** foar man tah bahr·nehn meed
Is it safe for kids?	**Är det barnsäkert?** air det bahrn·sair·kert

Fun with Kids

Can you recommend something for kids?	**Kan du föreslå något för barn?** kan deu furr·reh·sloa noa·goht furr bahrn
Is it suitable for… year olds?	**Passar det för…-åringar?** pas·ar dee furr…oa·rihng·ar

▶For numbers, see page 184.

You May Hear...

Vad gullig! vahd geul·ig	How cute!
Vad heter *han/hon*? vahd hee·tehr *han/hoan*	What's *his/her* name?
Hur gammal är *han/hon*? heur gam·al air *han/hoan*	How old is *he/she*?

Basic Needs for Kids

Do you have...?	**Har ni...?** hahr nee...
– a baby bottle	**– en nappflaska** ehn nap·flas·ka
– baby wipes	**– våtservetter för barn** voat·ser·veht·er furr bahrn
– a car seat	**– en bilbarnstol** ehn beel·bahrn·stoal
– a children's *menu/portion*	**– en *barnmeny/portion*** ehn *bahrn·meh·new/pohrt·shoan*
– a highchair	**– en barnstol** ehn bahrn·stoal
– a crib [child's cot]	**– en barnsäng** ehn bahrn·sehng
– diapers [nappies]	**– blöjor** blury·ohr
– formula	**– välling** vehl·ihng
– a pacifier [soother]	**– en napp** ehn nap
– a playpen	**– ett lekrum** eht leek·ruhm
– a stroller [pushchair]	**– en sittvagn** ehn siht·vangn
Can I breastfeed the baby here?	**Får jag amma barnet här?** foar yahg ah·ma bahr·neht hair
Where can I change the baby?	**Var kan jag byta på babyn?** vahr kan yahg bew·ta poa bai·been

▶For dining with kids, see page 64.

Babysitting

Can you recommend a reliable babysitter? **Kan du rekommendera en pålitlig barnvakt?** kaun deu re•koh•mehn•dee•rahra ehn poa•leet•lihg bahrn•vakt

What's the charge? **Vad kostar det?** vahd kos•tar dee

I'll pick them up at... **Jag hämtar dem...** yahg hehm•tar dehm...

▶For time, see page 186.

I can be reached at... **Du kan nå mig på...** deu kan noa may poa...

Health and Emergency

Can you recommend a pediatrician? **Kan du rekommendera en barnläkare?** kan deu reh•koh•men•dee•ra ehn bahrn•lairk•a•rer

My child is allergic to... **Mitt barn är allergiskt mot...** miht bahrn air a•lehr•gisk moat...

My child is missing. **Mitt barn har kommit bort.** miht bahrn hahr koh•miht bohrt

Have you seen a *boy/girl*? **Har du sett en *pojke/flicka*?** hahr deu seht ehn *poy•ker/flih•ka*

▶For food items, see page 95.

▶For health, see page 171.

▶For police, see page 169.

For the Disabled

Essential

Is there...?	**Finns det...?** fihns det...
– access for the disabled	**– ingång för rörelsehindrade** in•goang furr rur•rehl•seh•hihn•dra•der
– a wheelchair ramp	**– en rullstolsramp** ehn reul•stoals•ramp
– a handicapped- [disabled-] accessible toilet	**– en handikappanpassad toalett** ehn hand•ee•kap•an•pas•ad toa•ah•leht
I need...	**Jag behöver...** yahg beh•hur•ver...
– assistance	**– hjälp** yehlp
– an elevator [lift]	**– en hiss** ehn hihs
– a ground floor room	**– ett rum på bottenvåningen** eht ruhm poa boh•tehrn•voa•nihng•hen

Getting Help

I'm disabled.	**Jag är handikappad.** yahg air hand•ee•kap•ad
I'm deaf.	**Jag är döv.** yahg air durv
I'm *visually/hearing* impaired.	**Jag är *synskadad/hörselskadad.*** yahg air *sewn•skah•dad/hur•sel•skah•dad*
I'm unable to *walk far/use the stairs.*	**Jag kan inte *gå långt/gå i trappor.*** yahg kan ihn•ter *goa loangt/goa ee trap•ohr*
Can I bring my wheelchair?	**Kan jag ta med min rullstol?** kan yahg tah meed mihn ruhl•stoal
Are guide dogs permitted?	**Är det tillåtet med ledarhund?** air dee tihl•loa•teht meed leed•ar•huhnd
Can you help me?	**Kan du hjälpa mig?** kan deu yehl•pa may
Could you *open/hold* the door?	**Kan du *öppna/hålla upp* dörren?** kan deu *urp•na/hoa•la uhp* dur•rehn

▼ Resources

Emergencies

Essential

Help!	**Hjälp!** yelp
Go away!	**Ge er iväg!** yeh ehr ee•vairg
Stop thief!	**Stoppa tjuven!** stop•a shcheu•vehn
Get a doctor!	**Hämta en läkare!** hehm•ta ehn lair•ka•rer
Fire!	**Det brinner!** dee brihn•ehr
I'm lost.	**Jag har gått vilse.** yahg hahr goat vihl•ser
Can you help me?	**Kan du hjälpa mig?** kan deu yehl•pa may

Police

Essential

Call the police!	**Ring polisen!** rihng poa•lee•sehn
Where's the nearest police station?	**Var ligger närmaste polisstation?** vahr lih•gehr nair•mas•ter poo•lees•sta•shoan
There's been an accident.	**Det har hänt en olycka.** det hahr hehnt ehn oa•lewk•a
I've been attacked.	**Jag har blivit anfallen.** jahg hahr blee•viht an•fa•lehn
My child is missing.	**Mitt barn har kommit bort.** miht bahrn hahr koh•miht bohrt

I need...	**Jag behöver...** yahg beh•hur•vehr...
– an interpreter	**– en tolk** ehn tohlk
– to contact my lawyer	**– kontakta min advokat** kohn•tak•ta mihn ad•voh•kaht
– to make a phone call	**– ringa ett samtal** rihng•a eht sam•tahl
I'm innocent.	**Jag är oskyldig.** yahg air oa•shewl•dihg

You May Hear...

Fyll i blanketten, tack. fewl ee blan•keht•ehn tak	Please fill out this form.
Er legitimation, tack. ehr lehg•ee•tih•ma•shoan tak	Your identification, please.
***När/var* hände det?** *nair/vahr* hehn•dehr dee	*When/Where* did it happen?
Hur ser *han/hon* ut? hewr seer *han/hoan* eut	What does *he/she* look like?

Lost Property and Theft

I want to report...	**Jag vill anmäla...** yahg vihl an•mair•la...
– a mugging	**– ett överfall** eht ur•vehr•fal
– a rape	**– en våldtäkt** ehn vohld•tehkt
– a theft	**– ett rån** eht roan
I've been *robbed/ mugged.*	**Jag har blivit *rånad/överfallen.*** yahg hahr blee•viht *roa•nad/ur•vehr•fal•ehn*
I've lost...	**Jag har tappat...** yahg hahr tah•pat...

My…has been stolen.	**Någon har stulit…** noa·gohn hahr steu·liht…
– knapsack	**– min ryggsäck** mihn rewg·sehk
– bicycle	**– min cykel** mihn sew·kehl
– camera	**– min kamera** mihn kah·meh·ra
– *car/rental*	**– min *bil/hyrbil*** mihn *beel/hewr·beel*
– computer	**– min dator** mihn dah·tohr
– credit cards	**– mina kreditkort** mee·na kre·deet·koart
– jewelry	**– mina smycken** mee·na smew·ken
– money	**– mina pengar** mee·na pehng·ar
– passport	**– mitt pass** miht pas
– purse [handbag]	**– min portmonnä** mihn pohrt·mo·nai
– traveler's checks [cheques]	**– mina resecheckar** mee·na ree·seh·shehk·ar
– wallet	**– min plånbok** mihn ploan·boak

Health

Essential

I'm sick [ill].	**Jag är sjuk.** yahg air sheuk
I need an English-speaking doctor.	**Jag behöver en engelsktalande läkare.** yahg beh·hur·vehr ehn ehng·ehlsk·tahl·an·der lair·ka·rer
It hurts here.	**Det gör ont här.** dee yurr oant hair
I have a stomachache.	**Jag har ont i magen.** yahg hahr oant ee mah·gehn

Finding a Doctor

Can you recommend a *doctor/dentist*?	**Kan du rekommendera *en läkare/ tandläkare?*** kan deu reh•koh•mehn•dee•ra ehn *lair•ka•rer/tand•lair•ka•rer*
Can the doctor come to see me here?	**Kan doktorn komma och undersöka mig här?** kan dohk•torn koh•ma ohk eun•der•sur•ka may hair
What are their office hours?	**Vilka är deras öppettider?** vihl•ka air dee•ras ur•peh•tee•dehr
Can I make an appointment for…?	**Kan jag boka en tid…?** kan yahg boa•ka ehn teed…
– today	**– idag** ee•dahg
– tomorrow	**– imorgon** ee•mo•ron
– as soon as possible	**– så snart som möjligt** soa snahrt som mury•ligt
It's urgent.	**Det är brådskande.** dee air broas•kan•der

Symptoms

I'm...	**Jag...** yahg...
– bleeding	**– blöder** blur·dehr
– constipated	**– är förstoppad** air furr·stop·ad
– dizzy	**– har yrsel** hahr ewr·sehl
– nauseous	***– mår illa.*** *moar ihl·la*
– vomiting	***– kräks.*** *krairks*
It hurts here.	**Det gör ont här.** dee yurr oant hair
I have...	**Jag har...** yahg hahr...
– an allergic reaction	**– en allergisk reaktion** ehn a·lehr·gihsk ree·ak·shoan
– chest pain	**– ont i bröstet** oant ee brurs·teht
– an earache	**– ont i örat** oant ee ur·rat
– a fever	**– feber** fee·behr
– pain	**– ont** oant
– a rash	**– ett utslag** eht eut·slahg
– a sprain	**– en stukning** ehn steuk·nihng
– some swelling	**– en lätt svullnad** ehn leht sveul·nad
– a stomachache	**– ont i magen** oant ee mah·gehn
– sunstroke	**– solsting** soal·stihng
I've been sick [ill] for...days.	**Jag har varit sjuk i...dagar.** yahg hahr vah·riht sheuk ee...dah·gar

▶ For numbers, see page 184.

Health Conditions

I'm *anemic/diabetic.*	**Jag är *anemisk/diabetiker.*** yahg air *a•nee•mihsk/dee•a•beh•tih•ker*
I'm allergic to *antibiotics/penicillin.*	**Jag är allergisk mot *antibiotika/ penicillin.*** yahg air a•lehr•gihsk moat *an•tih•bee•**oa**•tee•ka/pehn•eh•si•leen*

▶For food items, see page 95.

I have…	**Jag har…** yahg hahr…
– arthritis	**– artrit** ar•treet
– *high/low* blood pressure	**– *högt/låg* blodtryck** *hurgt/loagt* bload•trewk
– asthma	**– astma** as•ma
– a heart condition	**– hjärtproblem** yairt•proa•bleem
I'm taking… (medicine).	**Jag tar…(medicin).** yahg tahr… (meh•dee•seen)

You May Hear…

Vad är det för fel? vahd air dee fur feel	What's wrong?
Var gör det ont? vahr yur dee oant	Where does it hurt?
Tar du någon annan medicin? tahr deu noa•gohn an•an meh•dih•seen	Are you taking any other medication?
Är du allergisk mot något? air deu a•lehr•gihsk moat noa•goht	Are you allergic to anything?
Öppna munnen. urp•na muhn•ehn	Open your mouth.
Andas djupt. an•das yeupt	Breathe deeply.
Du behöver åka till sjukhuset. deu beh•hur•vehr oa•ka tihl sjeuk•heu•seht	You need to go to the hospital.

Hospital

Please notify my family. **Var snäll och underrätta min familj.** vahr snehl ohk eun•der•rehta mihn fa•mily

I'm in pain. **Jag har ont.** yahg hahr oant

I need a *doctor/nurse*. **Jag behöver en *läkare/ sjuksköterska*.** yahg beh•hur•vehr ehn *lair•ka•rer/sheuk•shur•ter•ska*

When are visiting hours? **När är det besökstid?** nair air dee beh•surks•teed

I'm visiting... **Jag vill besöka...** yahg vihl beh•sur•ka...

Dentist

I've *broken a tooth/lost a filling*. **Jag har *brutit av en tand/tappat en plomb*.** yahg hahr *breu•tiht afv ehn tand/tap•at ehn plohmb*

This tooth hurts. **Den här tanden gör ont.** dehn hair tan•dehn yur oant

Can you fix this denture? **Kan du reparera den här tandprotesen?** kan deu reh•pa•ree•ra dehn hair tand•proh•tees•ehn

Gynecologist

I have *menstrual cramps/a vaginal infection*. **Jag har *mens värk/en vaginal infektion*.** yahg hahr *mens vehrk/ ehn va•gih•nahl ihn•fehk•shoan*

I missed my period. **Min mens har inte kommit.** mihn mehns hahr ihn•ter koh•miht

I'm on the Pill. **Jag tar p-piller.** yahg tahr pee•pihl•ler

I'm (not) pregnant. **Jag är (inte) gravid.** yahg air (ihn•ter) gra•veed

I haven't had my period for…months.	**Jag har inte haft mens på… månader.** yahg hahr ihn•ter haft mehns poa… moa•na•dehr

▶For numbers, see page 184.

Optician

I've lost…	**Jag har tappat…** yahg hahr tap•at…
– a contact lens	**– en kontaktlins** ehn kohn•takt•lihns
– my glasses	**– mina glasögon** mee•na glahs•ur•gohn
– a lens	**– en lins** ehn lihns

Payment and Insurance

How much does it cost?	**Hur mycket kostar det?** heur mew•ker kos•tar dee
Can I pay by credit card?	**Kan jag betala med kreditkort?** kan yahg beh•tah•la meed kreh•deet•koart
I have insurance.	**Jag har försäkring.** yahg hahr furr•sair•krihng
Can I have a receipt for my insurance?	**Kan jag få ett kvitto för mitt försäkringsbolag?** kan yahg foa eht kvih•toh furr miht furr•sair•krihngs•boa•lahg

Pharmacy [Chemist]

Essential

Where's the nearest pharmacy [chemist]?	**Var är närmaste apotek?** vahr air nair•mas•teh a•poa•teek
What time does the pharmacy [chemist] *open/close*?	**När *öppnar/stänger* apoteket?** nair *urp•nar/stehng•ehr* a•poa•tee•keht

What would you recommend for…?	**Vad kan du rekommendera för…?** vahd kan deu reh•koh•mehn•dee•ra furr…
How much should I take?	**Hur mycket ska jag ta?** heur mew•ker skah yahg tah
Can you fill [make up] this prescription for me?	**Kan ni göra iordning det här receptet åt mig?** kan nee yur•ra ee oard•nihng dee hair reh•sehp•teht oat may
I'm allergic to…	**Jag är allergisk mot…** yahg air a•lehr•gihsk moat…

In addition to filling prescriptions, **apotek** (pharmacies) sell over-the-counter medication as well as their own brands of toiletries and cosmetics. Almost all pharmacies are open on weekdays, but not all are open late in the evening or on weekends. Business hours vary considerably depending on the pharmacy. Generally, business hours are between 9 a.m. and 5 p.m. on weekdays. Locations with evening hours usually close around 9 p.m., and weekend hours are generally 10 a.m. to 4 p.m.

Dosage Instructions

How much should I take?	**Hur mycket ska jag ta?** heur mew•ker skah yahg tah
How many times a day should I take it?	**Hur många gånger om dagen ska jag ta det?** heur moang•a goang•er ohm dah•gehn skah yahg tah dee
Is it suitable for children?	**Är det lämpligt för barn?** air dee lehmp•lihgt furr bahrn
I'm taking… (medicine).	**Jag tar…(medicin).** yahg tahr… (meh•dee•seen)
Are there side effects?	**Ger det några biverkningar?** yehr dee noa•gra bee•vehrk•nihng•ar

You May See...

***EN GÅNG/TRE GÅNGER* PER DAG**	*once/three times* a day
TABLETTER	tablets
DROPPAR	drop
***FÖRE/EFTER/TILLSAMMANS MED* MÅLTIDER**	*before/after/with* meals
PÅ FASTANDE MAGE	on an empty stomach
ENDAST FÖR UTVÄRTES BRUK	for external use only

Health Problems

I'd like some medicine for...	**Jag behöver medicin mot...** yahg beh•hur•vehr meh•dih•seen moat...
– a cold	**– en förkylning** ehn furr•chewl•nihng
– a cough	**– hosta** hoas•ta
– diarrhea	**– diarré** dee•a•reh
– an insect bite	**– ett insektbett** eht in•sekt•beht
– motion [travel] sickness	**– åksjuka** oak•sheu•ka
– a sore throat	**– halsont** hals•oant
– a sunburn	**– solbränna** soal•brehn•a
– an upset stomach	**– ont i magen** oant ee mah•gehn

Basic Needs

I'd like...	**Jag skulle vilja ha...** yahg skuh•ler vihl•ya hah...
– acetaminophen [paracetamol]	**– acetominofen** a•seht•a•mihn•oa•fehn
– antiseptic cream	**– antiseptisk salva** an•tih•sehp•tihsk sal•va

– aspirin – **huvudvärkstabletter** heu·vuhd·vairks·ta·bleh·ter

– bandage – **gasbinda** gahs·bihn·da

– a comb – **kam** kam

– condoms – **kondomer** kohn·doa·mehr

– contact lens solution – **kontaktlinsvätska** kohn·takt·lins·veht·ska

– deodorant – **deodorant** dee·oa·deh·rant

– a hairbrush – **en hårborste** ehn hoar·bohrsh·ter

– hair spray – **hårspray** hoar·spray

– ibuprofen – **ibuprofen** ee·beu·proa·fehn

– insect repellent – **myggolja** mewg·ohl·ya

– a nail file – **en nagelfil** ehn nah·gehl·feel

– a (disposable) razor – **en (engångs)-rakhyvel** ehn (een·goangs)·rahk·**hew**·vehl

– razor blades – **rakblad** rahk·blahd

– sanitary napkins [pads] – **bindor** bin·dohr

– shampoo/ conditioner – **schampo/hårbalsam** sham·poa/h**oa**r·bal·sam

– soap – **tvål** tvoal

– sunscreen – **solskyddskräm** soal·shewds·krairm

– tampons – **tamponger** tam·poang·ehr

– tissue – **papper näsdukar** pa·pehrs·nairs·deu·kar

– toilet paper – **toalettpapper** toa·a·leht·pa·pehr

– a toothbrush – **tandborste** tand·bohr·ster

– toothpaste – **tandkräm** tand·krairm

▶ For baby products, see page 164.

Grammar

Regular Verbs

The present tense of regular verbs in Swedish is formed by adding either -**r** or -**er** to the stem. If the stem ends in **a**, add an -**r**, if it ends in a consonant add -**er**. The past tense is formed by adding either -**de** or -**te** to the basic form. If the basic form ends in a **p**, **t**, **k** or **s**, add -**te**, if not then add -**de**. The future is formed by adding the present tense of **ska** (will) + the verb in the infinitive. This applies to all persons (e.g., I, you, he, she, it, etc.). Following are the present, past and future forms of the verbs **att köpa** (to buy) and **att fråga** (to ask). The different conjugation endings are in bold.

	Present	Past	Future
att köpa (to buy)	köp**er**	köp**te**	ska köpa
att fråga (to ask)	fråga**r**	fråga**de**	ska fråga

Irregular Verbs

There are a number of irregular verbs in Swedish; these must be memorized. Like regular verbs, however, the irregular verb form remains the same, irrespective of person(s). Following are the present, past and future conjugations for a number of important, useful irregular verbs.

	Present	Past	Future
att vara (to be)	**är**	**var**	**ska vara**
att ha (to have)	**har**	**hade**	**ska ha**
att komma (to come)	**kommer**	**kom**	**ska komma**
att göra (to do)	**gör**	**gjorde**	**ska göra**
att gå (to go/walk)	**går**	**gick**	**ska gå**

sing. = singular, inf. = informal, pl. = plural

Nouns and Articles

The indefinite article (a, an) is expressed with **en** for common nouns and with **ett** for neuter nouns. Generally, common nouns are those that can be both feminine and masculine (e.g. people, animals, etc.); neuter nouns have no gender (e.g. house, roof, etc.). However, there are several exceptions to this rule.

In Swedish, there are five different endings used to form plural nouns; three correspond to common gender nouns and two to neuter gender nouns. The following rules apply to nouns in the indefinite singular.

1. **en** words that end in -**a** take an -**or** ending
2. **en** words that end in -**e** take an -**ar** ending
3. **en** words with stress on the last vowel take an -**er** ending
4. **ett** words that end in a vowel take an -**n** ending
5. **ett** words that end in a consonant take no additional ending

Common gender nouns that end in a consonant are not covered by the rules above. These words will take either an -**ar** ending or an -**er** ending. The nouns which fall into this category will simply need to be memorized.

Singular indefinite	Plural indefinite
en flicka (a girl)	**flick<u>or</u>**
en timme (an hour)	**timm<u>ar</u>**
en telefon (a telephone)	**telefon<u>er</u>**
ett konto (an account)	**kont<u>on</u>**
ett hus (a house)	**hus**
en bil (a car)	**bil<u>ar</u>**

Definite articles: where in English we say "the car", the Swedes say the equivalent of "car-the", i.e. they tag the definite article onto the end of the noun. In the singular, common nouns take an -**en** ending, neuter nouns an -**et** ending. In the plural, common nouns add an -**na** and neuter nouns take an -**en** ending, neuter nouns an

-**et** ending. In the plural, common nouns add an -**na** and neuter nouns take an -**en**.

	Singular		Plural	
common gender	**katten**	the cat	**katterna**	the cats
neuter gender	**tåget**	the train	**tågen**	the trains

Pronouns

I	**jag**	it (common/neuter)	**den/det**
you (sing.,inf.)	**du**	we	**vi**
he	**han**	you (pl.)	**ni**
she	**hon**	they	**de**

In Swedish there are two terms for "you": **du** (singular/informal) and **ni** (plural/informal). Both are used when talking to relatives, friends, colleagues, children, between young people and in work situations. The plural form, **ni**, is used in other, more formal situations to refer to one or more persons. Its use has become less frequent, and is used only in very formal contexts. Nowadays you will hear most people address each other with **du**.

Word Order

Swedish is similar to English in terms of word order for simple sentences: It follows the subject-verb-object pattern.

Example:

Sara läser en bok. Sara is reading a book.

When the sentence doesn't begin with a subject, the word order changes; the verb and the subject are inverted.
Example:

Nu läser Sara en bok. Now Sara is reading a book.

However, **nu** (nu) could just as well be placed at the end of the sentence, e.g. **Sara läser en bok nu.**

Questions are formed by reversing the order of the subject and verb:

Du ser katten.	You see the cat.
Ser du katten?	Do you see the cat?

Negation

A statement can be negated by inserting the word **inte** after the verb:

Jag talar svenska.	I speak Swedish.
Jaga talar inte svenska.	I do not speak Swedish.

Demonstrative Adjectives

	Common	Neuter	Plural
this/these	**denna**	**detta**	**dessa**
that/those	**den**	**det**	**de**
	denna bil (this car)	**detta hus** (this house)	

Possessive Adjectives

	Common	Neuter	Plural
my	**min**	**mitt**	**mina**
your (sing.)	**din**	**ditt**	**dina**
our	**vår**	**vårt**	**våra**
his	**hans**		
hers		**hennes**	
its		**dess/dess**	
their		**deras**	
your (pl.)	**er**	**ert**	**era**

Adverbs and Adverbial Expressions

Adverbs are generally formed by adding **-t** to the corresponding adjective.

Hon går snabbt.	She walks quickly.
Hon har en snabb tempo.	She has a quick pace.

Essential

0	**noll** nohl
1	**ett** eht
2	**två** tvoa
3	**tre** tree
4	**fyra** few·ra
5	**fem** fehm
6	**sex** sehx
7	**sju** sheu
8	**åtta** oh·ta
9	**nio** nee·oa
10	**tio** tee·oa
11	**elva** ehl·va
12	**tolv** tohlv
13	**tretton** treh·tohn
14	**fjorton** fyeur·tohn
15	**femton** fehm·tohn
16	**sexton** sehx·tohn
17	**sjutton** sheu·tohn
18	**arton** ar·tohn
19	**nitton** nih·tohn
20	**tjugo** shcheu·goa
21	**tjugoett** shcheu·goa·eht
22	**tjugotvå** shcheu·goa·tvoa
30	**trettio** treh·tee·oa

31	**trettioett** treh·tee·oa·eht
40	**fyrtio** fuhr·tee·oa
50	**femtio** fehm·tee·oa
60	**sextio** sehx·tee·oa
70	**sjuttio** sheu·tee·oa
80	**åttio** oh·tee·oa
90	**nittio** nih·tee·oa
100	**hundra** huhn·dra
101	**hundraett** huhn·dra·eht
200	**två hundra** tvoa huhn·dra
500	**fem hundra** fehm huhn·dra
1,000	**ett tusen** eht teu·sehn
10,000	**tio tusen** tee·oa teu·sehn
1,000,000	**en miljon** ehn mihl·yoan

Ordinal Numbers

first	**första** furs·ta
second	**andra** an·dra
third	**tredje** tree·dyer
fourth	**fjärde** fyair·der
fifth	**femte** fehm·ter
once	**en gång** ehn goang
twice	**två gånger** tvoa goang·ehr
three times	**tre gånger** tree goang·ehr

Essential

What time is it?	**Hur mycket är klockan?** heur mew•ker air kloh•kan
It's noon [midday].	**Klockan är tolv.** kloh•kan air tolv
Midnight.	**Midnatt.** meed•nat
From 9 o'clock to 5 o'clock.	**Från nio till sjutton.** froan nee•oa tihl sheu•tohn
It's twenty after [past] four.	**Den är tjugo över fyra.** dehn air shcheu•goa ur•ver few•ra
It's a quarter to nine.	**Den är kvart i nio.** dehn air kvart ee nee•oa
5:30 a.m.	**Halv sex på morgonen.** halv sehx poa mor•oh•nehn
5:30 p.m.	**Halv sex på kvällen.** halv sehx poa kveh•lehn

Sweden officially follows the 24-hour clock. Formal communication, such as public transporation schedules and TV programming, follows this system. However, in ordinary conversation, time is generally expressed as shown above, often with the addition of **på morgonen** (in the morning), **på förmiddagen** (mid-morning), **på eftermiddagen** (in the afternoon), **på kvällen** (in the evening) and **på natten** (at night).

Days

Essential

Monday	**måndag** moan·dahg
Tuesday	**tisdag** tees·dahg
Wednesday	**onsdag** oans·dahg
Thursday	**torsdag** toash·dahg
Friday	**fredag** free·dahg
Saturday	**lördag** lurr·dahg
Sunday	**söndag** surn·dahg

Dates

yesterday	**igår** ee·goar
today	**idag** ee·dahg
tomorrow	**imorgon** ee·mo·ron
day	**dag** dahg
week	**vecka** veh·ka
month	**månad** moa·nad
year	**år** oar

Months

January **januari** ya•neu•ah•ree

February **februari** fehb•reu•ah•ree

March **mars** mash

April **april** ap•rihl

May **maj** maiy

June **juni** yeu•nee

July **juli** yeu•lee

August **augusti** a•guhss•tee

September **september** sehp•tehm•behr

October **oktober** ohk•toa•behr

November **november** noh•vehm•behr

December **december** dee•sehm•behr

Seasons

spring **vår** voar

summer **sommar** soh•mar

fall [autumn] **höst** huhst

winter **vinter** vihn•tehr

Holidays

January 1, New Year's Day **Nyårsdagen**

January 6, Epiphany **Trettondagen**

May 1, May Day **Första maj**

June 6, Flag Day **Flaggans dag**

December 25, Christmas Day **Juldagen**

December 26, Boxing Day **Annandag jul**

Movable Dates:

Good Friday	**Långfredagen**
Ascension	**Kristi himmelfärdsdag**
Whitsunday	**Pingstdagen**
All Saints' Day	**Allhelgonadagen**
Midsummer Day	**Midsommardagen**

The two most important holidays in Sweden are Midsummer and Christmas. **Midsommardagen** (Midsummer) is celebrated with midsummer poles (similar to the may pole) and traditional songs and dances. Traditional food includes **matjesill** (pickled herring), fresh fish and schnapps. For **Juldagen** (Christmas), special cakes and other delicious treats are prepared, such as **pepparkakor** (ginger cookies), **saffranbullar** (saffron buns) and **julbord** (Christmas **smörgåsbord**, a festive buffet). Though not an official holiday, **Luciadagen** (St. Lucia Day) on December 13 marks the beginning of the Chirstmas season. Swedes also celebrate the beginning of spring on April 30, which is known as **Valborgsmässoafton**, with huge bonfires, fireworks and singing. June 6 is **Flaggans dag** (Flag Day), the national day of Sweden. Street are decorated with yellow and blue, the colors of the Swedish flag, patriotic speeches are made and traditional games and meals are enjoyed.

Conversion Tables

Mileage

1 km – 0.62 mi	20 km – 12.4 mi
5 km – 3.10 mi	50 km – 31.0 mi
10 km – 6.20 mi	100 km – 61.0 mi

Measurement

1 gram	**gram** khrahm	= 0.035 oz.
1 kilogram (kg)	**kilogram** kee·loa·khrahm	= 2.2 lb
1 liter (l)	**liter** lee·tuhr	= 1.06 U.S./ 0.88 Brit. quarts
1 centimeter (cm)	**centimeter** sehn·tee· may·tuhr	= 0.4 inch
1 meter (m)	**meter** may·tuhr	= 3.28 feet
1 kilometer (km)	**kilometer** kee·loa·may·tuhr	= 0.62 mile

Temperature

-40° C – -40° F	-5° C – 23° F	15° C – 59° F
-30° C – -22° F	-1° C – 30° F	20° C – 68° F
-20° C – -4° F	0° C – 32° F	25° C – 77° F
-10° C – 14° F	5° C – 41° F	30° C – 86° F
	10° C – 50° F	35° C – 95° F

Oven Temperature

100° C – 212° F	177° C – 350° F
121° C – 250° F	204° C – 400° F
149° C – 300° F	260° C – 500° F

Useful Websites

www.sweden.se
The Swedish Institute

www.stockholmtown.com
Stockholm Visitors Board

www.goteborg.com
Göteborg tourist Office

www.sj.se
SJ, Swedish State Railway

www.sl.se
Public Transportation in Stockholm

www.svenskaturistforeningen.se
The Swedish Tourist Club

www.sob.nu
Swedish Mountain Guide Association

www.gangsport.com
Swedish Walking Association

www.svenska-cykelsallskapet.se
Swedish Cycling Association

www.sjofartsverket.se
Swedish Maritime Administration

www.musikfestivaler.se
Information on music festivals in Sweden

www.hihostels.com
Hostelling International website

www.berlitzpublishing.com
Berlitz Publishing website

English–Swedish Dictionary

A

about (approximately) omkring
accept *v* acceptera
accident olycka
accommodation logi
acetaminophen paracetamol
across över
acupuncture akupunktur
adapter adapter
address *n* adress
adopt *v* adoptera
after efter
age ålder
air conditioning luftkonditionering
air mail flygpost
airline flygbolag
airport flygplats
aisle seat plats i mittgången
all alla
allergic allergisk
allergic reaction allergisk reaktion
allergy allergi
allow *v* tillåta
alter *v* ändra på
alternate route annan väg
aluminum foil aluminiumfolie
a.m. fm
ambulance ambulans
amount summa
amusement park nöjesfält
and och
anemic anemisk
animal djur
another annan
antiques store antikaffär
antiseptic cream antiseptisk salva
anyone någon
anything något
apartment lägenhet
apologize *v* be om ursäkt
appliance apparat
approve *v* godkänna
area code riktnummer
aromatherapy aroma-terapi
arrival ankomst
arrive *v* anlända
ask *v* fråga
aspirin huvudvärkstablett
asthma astma
at vid
ATM Bankomat
attack *n* anfall
audio guide audioguide
authentic äkta
automatic automatisk
available ledig
away iväg

adj	adjective	**adv**	adverb	**BE**	British English
n	noun	**v**	verb		

B

baby baby
baby bottle nappflaska
baby formula välling
baby wipes våtservetter för barn
babysitter barnvakt
backpack ryggsäck
bad dålig
bag (shopping) påse
baggage cart bagagekärra
baggage claim bagageutlämning
bakery bageri
band (music group) band
bandage (gauze) gasbinda
bank bank
bank charge bankavgift
banknote sedel
bar bar
barber herrfrisör
bath bad
bathroom badrum; **(toilet)** toalett
battery batteri
battlefield slagfält
be *v* vara
beach strand
beautiful vacker
become *v* bli
bed *n* säng
before före
begin *v* börja
behind bakom
belt skärp
between mellan
big stor
bicycle cykel
bicycle lock cykelås
bikini bikini
bill *n* **(restaurant bill)** nota; **(hotel, invoice)** räkning
birthday födelsedag
bite *n* bett; *v* **(bite)** bita; *v* **(chew)** tugga
black svart
blanket *n* täcke
bleed *v* blöda
blood blod
blood pressure blodtryck
blouse blus
board *v* **(flight)** borda
boarding house pensionat
boarding pass (airport) boardingkort
boat båt
boat tour båttur
book bok
bookstore bokhandel
boots stövlar
boring trist
botanical garden botanisk trädgård
bottle flaska
bottle opener flasköppnare
bowl djup tallrik
boy pojke
boyfriend pojkvän
bra behå
bracelet armband
break *v* gå sönder
breakdown *v* **(car)** gå sönder
breastfeed *v* amma
breathe andas

bridge bro
bring ta med
broken (broken) sönder; **(damaged)** trasig
brooch brosch
broom sopborste
brown brun
burn *v* brinna
bus buss
bus route busslinje
bus station bussterminal
bus stop busshållplats
business center businesscenter
business hours öppettider
business trip affärsresa
busy upptagen
but men
buy *v* köpa

C

cabin stuga
cafe kafé
calender kalender
call *v* **(phone)** ringa
calm lugn
camera kamera
camping bed tältsäng
can *n* burk; *v* **(be able to)** kan
can opener konservöppnare
cancel *v* avbeställa
car bil
car deck (ferry) bildäck
car ferry bilfärja
car park [BE] parkeringsplats
car rental biluthyrning
car seat bilbarnstol
carafe karaff
card *n* kort
carry on *n* **(luggage)** handbagage
cash kontant
cashier (male) kassör; **(female)** kassörska
casino kasino
castle slott
cathedral katedral
cave grotta
cell phone mobiltelefon
ceramics keramik
certificate of authenticity äkthetsbevis
chair lift stollift
change *n* **(money)** växel; *v* **(transportation; a baby)** byta; *v* **(reservation)** ändra;
cheap billig
check in *v* checka in
check in desk (airport) incheckning
check out *v* checka ut
checking account checkkonto
chemical toilet kemisk toalett
chemist [BE] apotek
chest bröstet
child barn
child's cot [BE] barnsäng
children's menu barnmeny
church kyrka
cigar cigarr
cinema [BE] bio

city (city) stad;
(downtown) centrum
city map stadskarta
classical music klassiskmusik
clean *n* ren
cleaning supplies städutrustning
clear *v* **(computer)** rensa
cliff klippa
cling film [BE] plastfolie
clock klocka
close *v* stänga
closed stängt
clothing store klädaffär
coat rock
coffee shop konditori
coin mynt
cold (illness) förskylning;
(temperature) kall
colleague kollega
color färg
comb kam
come *v* komma
company (business) firma;
(companionship) sällskap
computer dator
concert konsert
conditioner hårbalsam
condom kondom
conference konferens
conference room konferensrum
confirm *v* **(reservation)** bekräfta
contact lens solution kontaktlinsvätska
contain *v* innehålla
contraceptive preventivmedel
convention hall kongresshall
cooking facilities kokmöjligheter
cool (temperature) sval
copy *n* kopia
copy machine kopieringsautomat
corkscrew korkskruv
correct rätt
cost *v* kosta
cotton bomull
cough *n* hosta; *v* hosta
country code landsnummer
cover charge kuvertavgift
credit card kreditkort
crib barnsäng
cross country skiing längdåkning
crystal (glass) kristallglas
cup kopp
culture kultur
currency valuta
currency exchange office växelkontor
customs tull
customs declaration form tulldeklaration
cute *adj* gullig
cycling cykelåkning

D

dala horse dalahäst
damage *v* **(damage)** skada;
n **(harm)** skada
dance *v* dansa
dance club diskotek
day ticket dagsbiljett
day trip dagstur
deaf döv

debit card bankkort
declare *v* **(customs)** förtulla
deck chair solstol
deep djup
delay *n* försening
delete *v* **(computer)** radera
delicatessen delikatessaffär
denim denim
dentist tandläkare
denture tandprotes
deodorant deodorant
depart *v* **(train)** avgå
department store varuhus
departure (airport) avgång
departure gate avgångsgate
deposit handpenning
desire *adj* gärna; *n* lust
detour trafikomläggning
develop *v* **(photos)** framkalla
diabetic *n* diabetiker
dial *v* **(number)** slå
diamond diamant
diaper blöja
diarrhea diarré
diesel diesel
difficult svårt
digital digital
digital print digitalt kort
dirty smutsig
disabled rörelsehindrad
disabled accessible toilet [BE] handicappanpassad toalett
discount rabatt
discount card rabattkort
dish detergent diskmedel
dishwasher diskmaskin
display case vitrin
disposable camera engångskamera
disturb *v* störa
dive *v* dyka
divide *v* dela
diving equipment dykarutrustning
divorced skild
dizzy yr
do *v* **(do something)** göra; **(work with)** syssla med
do not disturb var god stör ej
doctor doktor
doll docka
dollar dollar
domestic (travel) inrikes
domestic flight inrikes flyg
domestic partner sambo
door dörr
dosage dosering
downtown centrum
dress klänning
dress code klädsel
drive *v* köra
driver's license körkort
drops (medication) droppar
dry cleaner kemtvätt
dubbed dubbad
duty free taxfri
duty free good taxfri vara

E

each varje
ear öra

earring örhänge
east öster
easy lätt
eat *v* äta
economy class turist klass
electrical outlet nätuttag
elevator hiss
e-mail e-post
e-mail address e-postadress
emergency nödsituation
emergency brake nödbroms
emergency exit nödutgång
English engelska
engrave *v* gravera
enter *n* **(entrance)** ingång; **(computer)** enter
entertainment underhållning
equipment utrustning
escalator rulltrappa
e-ticket e-biljett
European Union (EU) europeiska unionen
event händelse
examine *v* **(medical)** undersöka
excess baggage överviktsbagage
exchange rate växelkursen
excuse me (attention, pardon) ursäkta; **(to get past)** ursäkta mig
exit *n* **(way out)** utgång
expensive dyr
expert avancerad
express express
express mail expresspost
extension (phone) anknytning
eyeglasses glasögon

F

fabric tyg
family familj
fan (ventilation) fläkt
fantastic *adj* fantastisk
fare biljettpris
farm bondgård
fast fort
fax fax
fax machine fax machine
female kvinna
ferry färja
fever feber
field fält
fill *v* **(prescription)** göra i ordning
filling (dental) plomb
film [BE] film
fire exit brandutgång
first första
fishing fiske
fit *v* **(clothing)** passa
fitting room provrum
fix *v* laga
fixed price fast pris
flat [BE] lägenhet
flight flyg
flight number flygnummer
floor (level) våning
football [BE] fotboll
for (someone) för
foreign currency utländsk valuta
forest skog
forget *v* glömma
fork gaffel

form *n* blankett
fountain fontän
free (available) ledig
free of charge gratis
freezer frys
friend vän
from ifrån
frying pan stekpanna
fun rolig
function *v* **(work)** fungera
further (more) ytterliggare

G

game spel
garbage sopor
garbage bag soppåse
gasoline bensin
gas station bensinstation
gate (boarding) gate
genuine äkta
get off (train) stiga av
gift shop presentaffär
gift present
girlfriend flickvän
give *v* ge
glass (drinking) glas
gold guld
golf golf
golf club golfklubba
golf course golfbana
good *adj* bra
goodbye hej då
greengrocer [BE] livsmedelsaffär
grocery store livsmedelsaffär
group grupp
guest gäst
guide (brochure) guide; **(person)** guide
guide dog ledarhund
gym gym

H

hair cut klippning
hair dryer hårtork
hair style frisyr
hairbrush hårborste
hairdresser damfrisör
hairspray hårspray
half halv
handbag [BE] handväska
handicapped rörelsehindrade
handicapped accessible toilet handicappanpassad toalett
handicraft hantverk
handmade handgjord
hat hatt
have *v* ha
health food store hälsokostaffär
hearing impaired hörselskadad
heat värme
helmet hjälm
help *n* hjälp; *v* hjälpa
here här
hi hej
highchair barnstol
highway motorväg
hike *v* vandra
hiking vandring
hill kulle
hire *v* **[BE]** rent

holiday [BE] (vacation) semester
holiday (celebration) helgdag
horseback riding ridsport
hospital sjukhus
hot varm
hotel hotell
hour timme
husband man

I

ibuprofen ibuprofen
ice hockey ishockey
identification (idenitification) legitimation; **(ID card)** ID-kort
ill [BE] sjuk
in i
included (in the price) inkluderad
indoor pool inomhusbassäng
information desk information
innocent oskyldig
insect insekt
insect bite insektbett
insect repellent mygg olja
inside inuti
instant messenger instant messenger
instructor instruktör
insurance försäkring
interesting intressant
international (travel) utrikes
international driver's license internationellt körkort
internet internet
internet cafe internetkafé
interpreter tolk
iron *n* **(clothes)** strykjärn; *v* **(clothes)** stryka
itemized bill specificerad räkning

J

jacket jacka
jeans jeans
jet ski jetski
jeweler juvelerare
jewelry smycken
job jobb

K

keep *v* behålla
key nyckel
key card nyckelkort
kiddie pool barnbassäng
kiss *v* kyssa
kitchen kök
knife kniv
krona (Swedish currency) krona

L

lace spets
lactose intolerant laktosinterant
ladies' restroom damtoilett
ladieswear damkläder
lake sjö
last sista
late sen
launderette [BE] snabbtvätt
laundromat snabbtvätt
laundry tvätt
laundry detergent tvättmedel

laundry facilities tvättmöjligheter
lawyer advokat
leather läder
leave *v* lämna
left (direction) vänster
lesson lektion
letter brev
library bibliotek
life boat livbåt
life jacket flytväst
lifeguard livräddare
lift (ski) lift
lift [BE] *n* **(elevator)** hiss
lift pass liftkort
light (lamp) lampa
light bulb glödlampa
lighter tändare
like *v* gilla
line (bus) linje
linen linne
live *v* bo
loafers loafers
lock *v* låsa
log on logga in
log out logga ut
long *adj* lång; *adv* länge
lose *v* **(lost luggage)** förlora; *v* **(drop, lose)** tappa
lost *n* vilse
lost property office [BE] hittegodsexpedition
lost and found hittegodsexpedition
lottery lotto
love *v* älska
luggage locker förvaringsskåp

M

mail post
mailbox postlåda
manager chef
manicure manikyr
many många
map karta
market marknad
married gift
mass mässan
match (fire) tändsticka
meal måltid
mean *v* **(signify)** betyda
measuring spoon måttsked
medicine medicin
medium medium
meet *v* träffa
meeting sammanträde
memory card minneskort
men's restroom herrtoalett
menstrual cramps mensvärk
menstruation mens
menswear herrkläder
menu meny
message meddelande
microwave mikrovågsugn
minimum (requirement) minimum
Miss fröken
mistake misstag
mobile phone [BE] mobiltelefon
moment ögonblick
mop *n* skurmop
moped moped
mosque moské

motel motell
motion sickness åksjuka
motorboat motorbåt
motorcycle motocykel
motorway [BE] motorväg
mountain berg
mouth mun
movie film
movies bio
Mr. herr
Mrs. fru
mugging överfall
multi-day card flerdagskort
museum museum
must måste

N

nail file nagelfil
nail salon nagelvårdssalong
name *n* namn
napkin servett
nappy [BE] blöja
nature reserve naturreservat
nearby nära
necklace halsband
need *v* behöva
new ny
newspaper tidning
newsstand tidningskiosk
next nästa
next to bredvid
nice *adj* snäll
no (not allowed) ej
nobody ingen
no smoking rökning förbjuden
north norr
not inte
not included (in the price) inte inkluderad
nothing inget
number nummer
nurse sjuksköterska

O

off av
old gammal
on (switch) på
one way (street) enkelriktad
one-way ticket enkel biljett
only bara
open *n* öppet; *v* öppna
opening hours [BE] öppettider
opera opera
opposite mitt emot
optician optiker
or eller
orchestra orkester
order *v* beställa
other andra
outdoor utomhus
outdoor pool utomhusbassäng
outside ute
overnight delivery (mail) expressutdelning
oxygen treatment syrebehandling

P

pacifier napp
package paket
paddling pool [BE] barnbassäng

pajamas pyjamas
panorama panorama
pants byxor
panty hose strumpbyxor
paper napkin papperservett
parcel [BE] paket
park *n* park; *v* parkera
parking parkering
parking lot parkeringsplats
passport pass
passport control passkontroll
password (computer) lösenord
pay phone telefonautomat
pay *v* betala
peak (mountain) top
pearl pärla
pedestrian crossing övergångsställe för fotgängare
pedestrian fotgängare
pedicure pedikyr
pen kulspetspenna
per per
per day per dag
per week per vecka
performance (music, theater) föreställning
person person
petite petit
petrol [BE] bensin
petrol station [BE] bensinstation
pewter tenn
pharmacy apotek
phone call samtal
phone card telefonkort
phone number telefonnummer
photo foto
pick up *v* **(person/thing)** hämta
picnic area picknickområde
piece bit
pill tablett
pillow kudde
PIN PIN kod
pink rosa
piste [BE] spår
place *n* ställe
plan *n* plan
plaster [BE] plåster
plastic wrap plastfolie
platform (train) plattform
platinum platina
plate tallrik
play *n* **(theater)** teaterpjäs; *v* spela
playground lekplats
playpen lekrum
pleasant trevlig
please (request) snälla; **(invitation)** varsågod
plunger vaskrensare
pocket *n* ficka
point of interest sevärdhet
police polis
police report polisrapport
police station polisstation
pond damm
post office postkontor
postage porto
postcard vykort
pot (cooking pot) gryta; **(saucepan)** kastrull
pound sterling engelsk pund
pregnant gravid

premium (gas) premium
prescription recept
price pris
print (computer) skriva ut
private privat
private room privatrum
problem problem
produce store matbutik
program (events) program
pub pub
public transportation allmänna kommunikationer
pull dra
purple lila
purpose syfte
purse (large) handväska, **(small)** portmonnä
push tryck
pushchair [BE] sittvagn

R

racket (tennis) racket
railroad järnväg
railway [BE] järnväg
rain regn
raincoat regnkappa
rap rap
rape *n* våldtäkt
rapids fors
rash *n* utslag
(disposable) razor **(engångs)** rakhyvel
reach *v* nå
read *v* läsa
ready färdig
receipt kvitto
receive *v* ta emot
receptionist receptionist
recommend *v* rekommendera
refrigderator kylskåp
region region
regular gas vanlig
relationship (romantic) förhållande
rent *n* hyra; *v* hyra
repair *v* reparera
repairs (car) reparationer
repeat *v* upprepa
report *v* **(crime)** anmäla
reservation bokning
reserved reserverad
rest area rastplats
restroom (sign) WC
restaurant restaurang
return *v* **(give back)** återlämna
return ticket [BE] retur **(biljett)**
reverse charge call [BE] ba-samtal
right (correct) rätt; **(direction)** höger
ring (jewelry) ring
river flod
road väg
road map vägkarta
romantic romantisk
room rum
room service rumservice
round *n* **(golf)** runda
round-trip ticket retur biljett
rubbish [BE] sopor

S

safe *n* kassaskåp
sailing segling
sandals sandaler
sanitary napkin binda
saucepan kastrull
sauna bastu
save *v* **(collect)** spara
scarf halsduk
schedule tidsschema
scissors sax
sea hav
seat (on train) plats
seat number platsnummer
seat reservation (train) sittplatsbiljett
seminar seminarium
send *v* skicka
separated (couple) separerad
service serveringsavgift
service charge (bank) expeditionsavgift
sex sex
shampoo shampoo
sheet lakan
shoe store skoaffär
shoes skor
shopping basket shoppingkorg
shopping cart shoppingvagn
shopping centre [BE] shoppingcenter
shopping mall shoppingcenter
shorts shorts
show *v* visa
shower dusch
sick sjuk
side effect biverkning
sightseeing tour sightseeingtur
sign *v* undertäckna
silk siden
SIM card (cell phone) SIM kort
single ticket [BE] enkel **(biljett)**
sit *v* sitta
size storlek
skiing skidåkning
skirt kjol
slice *n* skiva
slippers tofflor
slippery (icy) hal
slow *adj* långsam
small liten
sneakers träningsskor
snorkeling equipment snorkelutrustning
snow snö
snowboard snowboard
snowshoes pjäxor
soap tvål
soccer fotboll
sock socka
something något
soon snart
soother [BE] napp
sore throat halsont
sorry förlåt
south söder
souvenir souvenir
spa spa
spatula stekspade
speak *v* tala
spoon sked

sports massage träningsmassage
spouse (female) maka; **(male)** make
sprain stukning
square (town feature) torg
stadium stadion
stair trappa
stamp *n* frimärke
stamp your ticket stämpla er biljett
start *v* **(car)** starta
stay *n* stanna
steakhouse stekhus
steep brant
stolen stulen
stomach magen
stomachache ont i magen
stop *n* **(bus stop)** bushållplats; *v* stanna
store *n* butik; *v* förvara
strange konstig
stream å
street gata
stroller sittvagn
student studerande
study *v* läsa
stunning jättesnygg
subtitle text
suburb förort
subway tunnelbana
subway station tunnelbanestation
suitable lämplig
suitcase resväska
sunburn solbränna
sunglasses solglasögon
sunstroke solsting
super [BE] (gas) premium
supermarket snabbköp
surfboard surfbräda
sweater tröja
sweatshirt sweatshirt
Swedish *adj* svensk; **(language)** svenska
swelling svullnad
swim *v* simma
swimming pool simbassäng
swimming trunks badbyxor
swimsuit baddräkt
symbol (computer) tecken
symphony (orchestra) symfoni
synagogue synagoga

T

table bord
tablecloth duk
take *v* ta
take out *v* ta ut
taken (occupied) upptagen
tampon tampong
tax skatt
taxi taxi
teaspoon tesked
temperature temperatur
temple tempel
tennis tennis
tennis court tennisbana
terminal (airport) terminal
terrible förskräcklig
text message sms
textiles textil
thank you tack

theft rån
thief tjuv
think *v* tänka
ticket biljett
ticket machine biljettautomat
ticket office biljettkontor
tie *n* slips
tights [BE] strumpbyxor
timetable [BE] tidsschema
tip (service) dricks
tissue näsduk
to till
tobacconist tobaksaffär
toilet [BE] toalett; **(sign)** WC
toilet paper toalettpapper
tooth tand
toothbrush tandborste
toothpaste tandkräm
tour tur
tourist turist
tourist attraction turistattraktion
tourist information turistinformation
tourist office turistbyrå
town hall stadshus
toy store leksaksaffär
track (railroad) spår
trail spår
train *n* tåg
train station järnvägsstation
tram spårvagn
translate *v* översätta
travel *v* **(travel)** resa; **(drive)** åka
travel agency resebyrå
travel agent (female) resebyråkvinna; **(male)** resebyråman
travel sickness [BE] åksjuka
traveler's check resecheck
traveller's cheque [BE] resecheck
treat *v* **(to a meal)** bjuda
trim (hair) putsning
trip *n* resa
trolley [BE] bagagekärra
trouser [BE] byxor
try *v* prova
turn off *v* stänga av
turn on *v* sätta på

U

ugly ful
umbrella (standard) paraply; **(sun)** solparasol
underground [BE] tunnelbana
underground station [BE] tunnelbanestation
understand *v* förstå
underwear (general) underkläder
unfortunately tyvärr
United Kingdom Storbritanien
unlimited (mileage) obegränsad
until tills
urgent brådskande
United State Förenta Staterna
use *v* använda
username användarnamn
utensil bestick

V

vacancy ledigt rum
vacation semester
vacuum cleaner dammsugare
vaginal infection vaginal infektion
valley dal
valuable värdesak
value *n* värde
vegetarian vegetarian
viewpoint utsiktspunkt
village by
visit *n* besök; *v* besöka
visiting hours besökstid
visitor besökare
visitor besökare
visually impaired syn skadad
vomit *v* kräkas

W

wait vänta
wake up *v* vakna
wake-up call telefonväckning
walk *n* promenad; *v* gå
wallet plånbok
want *v* vilja
washing machine tvättmaskin
waterfall vattenfall
weather forecast väderleksrapport
weekend helg
welcome välkommen
west väster
wheelchair rullstol
wheelchair ramp rullstolsramp
when när
where var
which vilken
white vitt
who vem
widow änka
widower änkling
window fönster
window seat fönsterplats
windsurfing vindsurfa
wireless internet trådlös internet
with med
withdrawal (bank) uttag
wood trä
wool ull
work from home *v* arbeta hemifrån
wrap *v* **(present)** slå in
write *v* skriva
wrong fel

Y

yellow gul
yes ja
yield lämna företräde
youth hostel vandrarhem

Z

zoo djurpark

Swedish–English Dictionary

A

acceptera *v* accept
adapter adapter
adoptera *v* adopt
adress *n* address
advokat lawyer
affärscentrum shopping mall [centre BE]
affärsresa business trip
akupunktur acupuncture
alla all
allergi allergy
allergisk allergic
allergisk reaktion allergic reaction
allmänna kommunikationer public transportation
alternativ väg alternate route
aluminiumfolie aluminum foil
ambulans ambulance
amma *v* breastfeed
andas breathe
andra other
anemisk anemic
anfall *n* attack
anknytning extension (phone)
ankomst arrival
anlända *v* arrive
anmäla *v* report (crime)
annan another
antikaffär antiques store
antiseptisk salva antiseptic cream
använda *v* use
användarnamn username
apotek pharmacy [chemist BE]
apparat appliance
arbeta hemifrån *v* work from home
armband bracelet
aroma-terapi aromatherapy
astma asthma
audioguide audio guide
automatisk automatic
av off
avancerad expert
avbeställa *v* cancel
avgå *v* depart (plane)
avgång departure
avgångsgate departure gate

B

baby baby
bad bath
badbyxor swim trunks
baddräkt swim suit
badrum bathroom [toilet BE]
bagagekärra baggage cart [trolley BE]
bagageutlämning baggage claim
bageri bakery
bakom behind
band band (music group)
bank bank
bankavgift bank charge
bankkort debit card

Bankomat ATM
bar bar
bara only (just)
barn child
barnbassäng kiddie pool [paddling pool BE]
barnmeny children's menu
barnstol highchair
barnsäng crib [child's cot BE]
barnvakt babysitter
bastu sauna
batteri battery
be om ursäkt *v* apologize
behå bra
behålla *v* keep
behöva *v* need
bekräfta *v* confirm (reservation)
bensin gasoline [petrol BE]
bensinstation gas station [petrol station BE]
berg mountain
bergklättring rock climbing
bestick utensil
beställa *v* order
besök *n* visit
besöka *v* visit
besökare visitor
besökstid visiting hours
betala *v* pay
bett *n* bite
betyda mean (signify)
bibliotek library
bikini bikini
bil car
bilbarnstol car seat
bildäck car deck (ferry)
bilfärja car ferry
biljett ticket
biljettautomat ticket machine
biljettkontor ticket office
biljettpris fare
billig cheap
bilsäte car seat
biluthyrning car rental
binda sanitary napkin [towel BE]
bio movies [cinema BE]
bit piece
bita *v* bite
biverkning side effect
bjuda *v* treat (to a meal)
blankett *n* form
bli *v* become
blod blood
blodtryck blood pressure
blus blouse
blöda bleed
blöja diaper [nappy BE]
bo *v* live
boardingkort boarding pass
bok book
bokhandel bookstore
bokning reservation (travel, restaurant)
bomull cotton
bondgård farm
bord table
borda *v* board (flight)
botanisk trädgård botanical garden
bra *adj* good

brandutgång fire exit
brant steep
bredvid next to
brev letter
brinna *v* burn
bro bridge
brosch brooch
brun brown
brådskande urgent
bröstet chest
burk *n* can
businesscenter business center
buss bus
busshållplats bus stop [request stop BE]
busslinje bus route
bussterminal bus station
butik *n* store
by village
byta *v* change (baby, connection)
byxor pants [trouser BE]
båt boat
båttur boat tour
börja *v* begin

C

centrum downtown
checka in check in (airport)
checka ut check out (hotel)
chef manager
cigarr cigar
cykel bicycle
cykelåkning cycling
cykelås bicycle lock

D

dagsbiljett day ticket
dagstur day trip
dal valley
dalahäst dala horse
damfrisör hairdresser
damkläder ladieswear
damtoalett ladies' restroom
damm pond
dammsugare vacuum cleaner
dansa *v* dance
dator computer
dela divide
delikatessaffär delicatessen
denim denim
deodorant deodorant
diabetiker *n* diabetic
diamant diamond
diarré diarrhea
diesel diesel
digital digital
digitalt kort digital print
diskmedel dish detergent
diskmaskin dishwasher
djup deep
djup tallrik bowl
djur animal
djurpark zoo
docka doll
doktor doctor
dollar dollar
dosering dosage
dra pull
dricks tip (service)

droppar drops (medication)
dubbad dubbed
duk table cloth
dusch shower
dyka *v* dive
dykarutrustning diving equipment
dyr expensive
dålig bad
dörr door
döv deaf

E

e-biljett e-ticket
efter after
ej no (do not...)
eller or
endast only (nothing but)
engelska English
engelsk pund pound sterling
engångskamera disposable camera
enkel biljett one-way trip [single ticket BE]
enkelriktad one way (street)
enter enter (computer)
e-post e-mail
e-postadress e-mail address
europeiska unionen European Union (EU)
expeditionsavgift service charge (bank)
express express
expresspost express mail
expressutdelning overnight delivery (mail)

F

familj family
fantastisk *adj* fantastic
fast pris fixed price
fax fax
fax machine fax machine
feber fever
fel wrong
ficka *n* pocket
film movie [film BE]
fiske fishing
flaska bottle
flasköppnare bottle opener
flerdagskort multi-day card
flickvän girlfriend
flod river
flyg flight
flygbolag airline
flygnummer flightnumber
flygplats airport
flygpost airmail
fläkt fan
fm a.m.
fontän fountain
fors rapids
fort fast
fotboll soccer [football BE]
fotgängare pedestrian
foto photo
framkalla *v* develop (photos)
fri free
frimärken stamps
frisyr hair style
fru Mrs.

frys freezer
fråga ask
från from...
fröken Miss
ful ugly
fungera *v* function (work)
fylla *v* fill
fält field
färdig ready
färg color
färja ferry
födelsedag birthday
fönster window
fönsterplats window seat
för tung/stor too much, excess (baggage)
före before
Förenta Staterna United States
föreställning performance (music, theater)
förhållande relationship (romantic)
förlora *v* lose
förlåt sorry
försening *n* delay
förskräcklig terrible
förskylning cold (sick)
första first
förstå *v* understand
försäkring insurance
förtulla *v* declare (customs)
förvaringsskåp luggage locker
förort suburb

G

gaffel fork
gammal *adj* old, *n* age
gasbinda bandage (gauze)
gata street
gate gate (boarding)
ge *v* give
gift married
gilla *v* like
glas glass (drinking)
glasögon eyeglasses
glödlampa light bulb
glömma *v* forget
godkänna *v* approve
golf golf
golfbana golf course
golfklubb golf club
gratis free of charge
gravera *v* engrave
gravid pregnant
grotta cave
grupp group
gryta pot (cooking)
guide guide (brochure); guide (person)
gul yellow
guld gold
gullig *adj* cute
gym gym
gå *v* walk, leave
gå sönder break; breakdown (car)
gärna *adj* desire
göra *v* do

H

ha *v* have
hal slippery (icy)
halsband necklace
halsduk scarf
halsont sore throat
halv halv
handbagage carry on
handgjord handmade
handicappanpassad toalett handicapped accessible toilet [disabled BE]
handpenning deposit
handväska purse [hand bag BE]
hantverk handicraft
hatt hat
hav sea
hej hi
hej då goodbye
helg weekend
helgdag holiday (celebration)
hemifrån work from home
hemlagad homemade (food)
herr Mr.
herrfrisör barber
herrkläder menswear
herrtoalett men's restroom
hiss elevator [lift BE]
hittegodsexpedition lost-and-found [lost property office BE]
hjälm helmet
hjälp *n* help
hjälpa *v* help
hosta *n* cough; *v* to cough
hotell hotel
huvudvärkstablett aspirin
hyra rent [hire BE]
hårbalsam conditioner
hårborste hairbrush
hårspray hairspray
hårtork hair dryer
hälsokostaffär health food store
hämta *v* pick up (thing/person)
händelse event
här here
höger right (direction)
hörselskadad hearing impaired

I

i in
ibuprofen ibuprofen
ID-kort identification
ifrån from
incheckning check in desk (airport)
information information desk
ingen nobody (sg)
inget nothing
ingång entrance
inkluderad included (in the price)
innehålla contain
inomhusbassäng indoor swimming pool
inrikes domestic (travel)
inrikes flyg domestic flight
insekt insect
insektbett insect bite
instant messenger instant messenger
instruktör instructor

inte not
inte inkluderad not included (in the price)
internationellt körkort international driver's license
internet internet
internetkafé internet cafe
intressant interesting
inuti inside
ishockey ice hockey
iväg away

J

ja yes
jacka jacket
jeans jeans
jetski jet ski
jobb job
juvelerare jeweler
järnväg railroad [railway BE]
järnvägsstation train station
jättesnygg stunning

K

kafé cafe
kalender calender
kall cold (temperature)
kam comb
kamera camera
kan *v* can (be able to)
karaff carafe
karta map
kasino casino
kassaskåp *n* safe
kassör cashier (male)
kassörska cashier (female)
kastrull saucepan (cooking)
katedral cathedral
kemisk toalett chemical toilet
kemtvätt dry cleaner
keramik ceramics
kjol skirt
klassiskmusik classical music
klippa cliff
klippning hair cut
klocka(n) clock
klädaffär clothing store
klädsel dress code
klänning dress
kniv knife
kokmöjligheter cooking facilities
kollega colleague
komma *v* come
konditori coffee shop
kondom condom
konferens conference
konferensrum conference room
kongresshall convention hall
konsert concert
konservöppnare can opener
konstig strange
kontaktlinsvätska contact lens solution
kontant *n* cash
kopia *n* copy
kopieringsautomat copy machine
kopp cup
korkskruv corkscrew
kort *n* card, *adj* short
kosta *v* cost

kostym suit (jacket/pants)
kreditkort credit card
kristallglas crystal (glass)
krona krona (Swedish currency)
kräkas *v* vomit
kudde pillow
kulle hill
kulspetspenna pen
kultur culture
kuvertavgift cover charge
kvinna female
kvitto receipt
kylskåp refridgerator
kyrka church
kyssa *v* kiss
kök kitchen
köpa *v* buy
köra drive
körkort driver's license

L

laga *v* fix
lakan sheet
laktosintolerant lactose intolerant
lampa light (lamp)
landsnummer country code
ledarhund guide dog
ledig available
ledigt rum vacancy
legitimation identification
lekplats playground
lekrum playpen
leksaksaffär toy store
lektion lesson
liftkort liftpass
lila purple
linje line
linne linen
liten small
livbåt life boat
livräddare lifeguard
livsmedelsaffär grocery store [greengrocer BE]
loafers loafers
logga in log on (connect to internet)
logga ut log out
logi accommodation
lotto lottery
luftkonditionering air conditioning
lugn calm
lust *n* desire
lyft lift (ski)
lång long
långsam slow
låsa *v* lock
läder leather
lägenhet apartment [flat BE]
lämna *v* leave
lämna före träde yield
lämplig suitable
längdåkning cross country skiing
länge long (time)
läsa *v* (book) read; (school) study
lätt easy
lösenord password

M

magen stomach
maka spouse (female)

make spouse (male)
man husband, man
manikyr manicure
marknad market
matbutik produce store (general store) [grocer BE]
med with
meddelande message
medicin medicine
medium medium
mellan between
men but
mens menstruation
mensvärk menstrual cramps
meny menu
mikrovågsugn microwave
minimum minimum (requirement)
minneskort memory card
misstag mistake
mitt emot opposite
mobiltelefon cell phone [mobile phone BE]
moms sales tax [VAT BE]
moped moped
moské mosque
motel motel
motorcykel motorcycle
motorbåt motorboat
motorväg highway [motorway BE]
mun mouth
museum museum
mygg olja insect repellent
mynt coin
måltid meal
många many
måste must
måttsked measuring spoon
mässan mass (catholic)

N

nagelfil nail file
nagelvårdssalong nail salon
namn *n* name
napp pacifer [soother BE]
nappflaska baby bottle
naturreservat nature reserve
norr north
nota bill (restaurant)
nummer number
ny new
nyckel key
nyckelkort key card
nå *v* reach
någon anyone
något anything, something
när when
nära nearby
näsduk tissue
nästa next
nätuttag electrical outlet
nödbroms emergency brake
nödsituation emergency
nödutgång emergency exit
nöjesfält amusement park

O

obegränsad unlimited (mileage)
och and
olycka accident

omkring about (approximately)
ont i magen stomachache
opera opera
optiker optician
orkester orchestra

P

paket package [parcel BE]
panorama panorama
papperservett paper napkin
paracetamol acetaminophen
paraply umbrella
park park
parkering parking
parkering på gatan street parking
parkeringsplats (one or several) parking lot [car park BE]
pass passport
passa *v* fit
passkontroll passport control
pedikyr pedicure
pensionat boarding house
per per
per dag per day
per vecka per week
person person
petit petite
picknickområde picnic area
PIN kod PIN code
pjäxor snowshoes
plan *n* plan
plastfolie plastic wrap [cling film BE]
platina platinum
plats seat (on train)
plats i mittgången aisle seat
platsnummer seat number
plattform platform (train)
plomb filling
plånbok wallet
pojke boy
pojkvän boyfriend
polis police
polisrapport police report
polisstation police station
porto postage
post mail
postkontor post office
postlåda mail box
premium premium [super BE] (gas)
presentaffär gift shop
present gift
preventivmedel contraceptive
pris price
privat private
privatrum private room
problem problem
program progam (events)
prova *v* try
provrum fitting room
pub pub
putsning trim (hair)
pyjamas pajamas
på on (switch)
påse bag
pärla pearl

R

rabatt discount
rabattkort discount card
racket racket (tennis)
radera delete (computer)
(engångs)rakhyvel (disposable) razor
rap rap
rastplats rest area
recept prescription
receptionist receptionist
region region
regn rain
regnkappa raincoat
rekommendera *v* recommend
ren adj clean
rensa clear (computer, ATM), clean
reparationer repairs (car)
reparera *v* repair
resa *v* travel, *n* trip
resebyrå travel agency
resebyråkvinna travel agent (female)
resebyråman travel agent (male)
resecheck traveler's check [traveller's cheque BE]
reserverad reserved
restaurang restaurant
resväska suitcase
retur (biljett) round-trip ticket [return ticket BE]
ridsport horseback riding
riktnummer area code
ring ring (jewelry)
ringa *v* call (phone)
rock coat
rolig fun
romantisk romantic
rosa pink
rullstol wheelchair
rullstolsramp wheelchair ramp
rulltrappa escalator
rum room
rumservice room service
runda *v* round (golf)
ryggsäck backpack
rån theft
räkning bill (hotel, invoice)
rätt correct
rökning förbjuden no smoking
rörelsehindrad disabled

S

sambo domestic partner
sammanträde meeting
samtal phone call
sandaler sandals
sax scissors
sedel banknote
segling sailing
semester vacation
seminarium seminar
sen late
separerad separated (couple)
serveringsavgift service
servett napkin
sevärdhet point of interest
sex sex

shampoo shampoo
shoppingcenter shopping mall [shopping centre BE]
shoppingkorg shopping basket
shoppingvagn shopping cart
shorts shorts
siden silk
sightseeingtur sightseeing tour
simbassäng swimming pool
SIM kort SIM card (cell phone)
simma *v* swim
sista last
sitta *v* sit
sittplatsbiljett seat reservation (train)
sittvagn stroller [pushchair BE]
sjuk sick [ill BE]
sjukhus hospital
sjuksköterska nurse
sjö lake
skada *n* damage, *v* harm
skatt tax
sked spoon
skicka *v* send
skidåkning skiing
skild divorced
skiva *n* slice
skoaffär shoe store
skog forest
skor shoes
skriva write
skriva ut print
skurmop *n* mop
skyldig innocent
skärp belt
slagfält battlefield
slips tie
slott castle
slå *v* (phone number) dial
slå in *v* wrap (present)
sms text message
smutsig dirty
smycken jewelry
snabbköp supermarket
snabbtvätt laundromat [launderette BE]
snart soon
snorkelutrustning snorkeling equipment
snowboard snowboard
snäll *adj* nice
snälla (request) please
snö snow
socka sock
solbränna sunburn
solglasögon sunglasses
solsting sunstroke
solstol deck chair
sopborste broom
sopor garbage (garbage disposal) [rubbish BE]
soppåse garbage bag
souvenir souvenir
spa spa
spara *v* save
specifierad räkning itemized bill
spel game
spela *v* play
spets lace
spår trail [piste BE]; track (railroad)

spårvagn tram
stad city
stadion stadium
stadshus town hall
stadskarta city map
stanna *n* stay; *v* stop
starta *v* start
stekhus steakhouse
stekpanna frying pan
stekspade spatula
stiga av get off (train)
stollift chair lift
stor big
Storbritannien United Kingdom
storlek size
strand beach
strumpbyxor panty hose [tights BE]
strykjärn iron (clothes)
studerande student
stuga cabin
stukning *n* sprain
stulen stolen
städutrustning cleaning supplies
ställe place
stämpla er biljett stamp your ticket
stäng av turn off
stänga *v* close
stängt closed
störa disturb
stövlar boots
summa amount
surfbräda surfboard
sval cool (temperature)
svart black
sweatshirt sweatshirt
svensk *adj* swedish
svenska *adj* swedish; (language) Swedish
svullnad swelling
svårt difficult
syfte purpose
symfoni symphony (orchestra)
syn skadad visually impaired
synagoga synagogue
syrebehandling oxygen treatment
syssla med *v* do (work with)
sällskap company (companionship)
säng bed
sätta på turn on
söder south
sönder broken

T

ta *v* take
ta emot *v* receive
ta med bring
ta ut take out
tablett pill (tablet)
tack thank you
tala *v* speak
tallrik plate
tampong tampon
tand tooth
tandborste toothbrush
tandkräm toothpaste
tandläkare dentist
tandprotes dentures

tappa *v* lose; drop
taxfri duty free
taxfri vara duty free good
taxi taxi
teaterpjäs play (theater)
tecken symbol (computer)
telefon katalog telephone catalog
telefonautomat pay phone
telefonkort phone card
telefonnummer phone number
telefonväckning wake up call
temperatur temperature
tempel temple
tenn pewter
tennis tennis
tennisbana tennis court
terminal terminal (airport)
tesked teaspoon
text subtitle
textil textiles
tidning newspaper
tidningskiosk newsstand
tidsschema schedule [timetable BE]
till to
tills until
tillåta *v* allow
timme hour
toalett bathroom [toilet BE]
toalettpapper toilet paper
tobaksaffär tobacconist
tofflor slippers
tolk interpreter
top peak (moutain)
torg square (town feature)
trappa stair
trasig broken (damaged)
trevlig pleasant
trist boring
tryck push
trådlös internet wireless internet
trä wood
träffa *v* meet
träfigur wood carvings
träkniv wooden knife
träningsmassage sports massage
träningsskor sneakers
träsked wooden spoon
träskor wooden clogs
tröja sweater
tugga *v* chew
tull customs
tulldeklaration customs declaration form
tunnelbana subway [underground BE]
tunnelbanestation subway station [underground station BE]
tur tour
turist tourist
turist klass economy class
turistattraktion tourist attraction
turistbyrå tourist office
turistinformation tourist information
tvål soap
tvätt laundry
tvättmaskin washing machine
tvättmedel laundry detergent

tvättmöjligheter laundry facilities
tyg fabric
tyvärr unfortunately
tåg train
täcke *n* blanket
tältsäng camping bed
tändare lighter
tändsticka match (fire)
tänka *v* think

U

ull wool
underhållning entertainment
underkläder underwear (general)
undersöka *v* examine (medical)
undertäckna *v* sign
upprepa *v* repeat
upptagen busy
ursäkta *v* excuse me (to get attention, pardon me)
ursäkta mig excuse me (to get past)
ute outside
utgång exit way out
utländsk valuta foreign currency
utomhus outdoor
utomhusbassäng outdoor pool
utrikes international (travel)
utrustning equipment
utsiktspunkt view point
utslag *n* rash
uttag withdrawal (bank)

V

vacker beautiful
vaginal infektion vaginal infection
vakna *v* wake up
valuta currency
vandra *v* hike
vandrarhem youth hostel
vandring hiking
vanlig regular gas
var where
var god stör ej do not disturb
vara *v* be
varje each
varm hot
varsågod (invitation) please
varuhus department store
vaskrensare plunger
vattenfall waterfall
WC (sign) restroom [toilet BE]
veckotidning magazine
vegetarian vegetarian
vem who
vid at
vilja *v* want
vilken which
vilse lost
visa *v* show
vitrin display case
vitt white
vykort postcard
våldtäkt *n* rape
våning floor (level, etage in building)

våtservetter för barn baby wipes
väderleksrapport weather forecast
väg road
vägkarta road map
välkommen welcome
välling baby formula
vän friend
vänster left (direction)
vänta wait
värde *n* value
värdesak *n* valuable
värme heat
väska bag
väster west
växel *n* change (money)
växelkontor currency exchange office
växelkursen exchange rate
växla change money

Y

yr dizzy
ytterliggare further (more)

Å

å stream
åka *v* travel, drive (motor vehicle)
åksjuka motion sickness [travel sickness BE]
ålder age
återlämna *v* return (give back)
äkta authentic
äkthetsbevis certificate of authenticity
älska *v* love
ändra *v* change (reservation)
ändra på *v* alter
änka widow
änkling widower
äta *v* eat

Ö

ögonblick (one) moment
öppet open
öppettider business hours [opening hours BE]
öppna *v* open
öra ear
öre öre (Swedish currency)
örhänge earring
öster east
över across (the road)
överfall mugging
övergångsställe för fotgängare pedestrian crossing
översätta *v* translate
överviktsbagage excess baggage